Study Guide

for Spielvogel's

WESTERN CIVILIZATION:

Fourth Edition

VOLUME II: Since 1550

James T. Baker
Western Kentucky University

Australia • Canada • Denmark • Japan • Mexico • New Zealand • Philippines
Puerto Rico • Singapore • South Africa • Spain • United Kingdom • United States

For more information, contact
Wadsworth/Thomson Learning
10 Davis Drive
Belmont, CA 94002-3098
USA
www.wadsworth.com

International Headquarters
Thomson Learning
290 Harbor Drive, 2nd Floor
Stamford, CT 06902-7477
USA

UK/Europe/Middle East
Thomson Learning
Berkshire House
168-173 High Holborn
London WC1V 7AA
United Kingdom

Asia
Thomson Learning
60 Albert Complex
Singapore 189969

Canada
Nelson/Thomson Learning
1120 Birchmount Road
Scarborough, Ontario M1K 5G4
Canada

ISBN 0-534-56843-2

CONTENTS

iv

PREFACE

This study guide was prepared to accompany the text *Western Civilization* by Jackson J. Spielvogel. The first volume, which includes Chapters 1-16, can be used in conjunction with *Volume I*. The second volume, which includes Chapters 14-29, can be used in conjunction with *Volume II*.

The guide contains seven types of exercises for each of the chapters:
a. Words to Identify—important names, places, ideas, works of literature, art, and music to know and understand
b. Words to Match with their Definitions—important terms to be matched with their meanings, a second form of identification
c. Multiple Choice Questions—20 of these for each chapter, a way of testing factual and conceptual learning
d. Sentences to Complete—with spaces provided that allow you to complete an interpretive statement with specific words and phrases
e. Chronological Arrangement—for each chapter a set of seven events which you place in chronological order and give their dates
f. Questions for Critical Thought—questions that ask you to recall and relate important concepts and prepare you for essay examinations
g. Analysis of Primary Source Documents—questions that ask you to apply the information presented in the boxes of each chapter, documents from the time period studied.

In addition, at the end of certain chapters, there are map exercises to test your knowledge of geography important to the various historical periods. You may check your completed maps with the appropriate ones in the text. Answers to exercises b, c, d, and e are found at the end of the guide.

You will probably be asked on your examinations to write essays. Essays not only test your knowledge of the facts but your ability to interpret and apply them. The exercises in this volume called Questions for Critical Thought and Analysis of Primary Source Documents should be of help to you in preparing for essay questions. In addition let me offer you several suggestions on how to write essays that will both teach you and help you make high marks:

a. Read the entire question, and be sure that you understand exactly what is being asked and that you consider all parts of it. Address yourself only to the question that is asked, but address yourself to every section of it.

b.   Make an outline before you begin to write the essay. Jot down in as few words as possible the major points you want to make, the most important persons, places, and ideas you want to include. Then glance back at your outline as you write so that you will not stay too long on one point or omit another.

c.   Try to make one major point in your essay, with all of the others subordinate to it. This is your thesis. State it at the beginning, refer back to it at various appropriate times, and restate it briefly at the end. This will keep you focused on a unifying theme.

d.   Write for an imaginary reader (who will be your teacher or an assistant, but you may not know exactly who it will be) who is intelligent but does not necessarily know the information you are relating. This way you will not fail to provide all information necessary to explain yourself, but you will also not insult your reader.

e.   Be careful to spell correctly and to use good grammar. A history course is not an English course, and graders may or may not "count off" for poor spelling and grammar; but all graders are impressed either positively or negatively by the quality of your mechanics. While you may not see a specific comment about such matters on your essay, you may be sure that they have affected your final grade.

f.   Think of an essay in a positive light. It should and can be an exercise in which the facts you have learned take focus and shape and make more sense than ever before. If done correctly, an essay can be the truest learning experience you can have and the most certain measure of your achievement.

I hope that this booklet adds to your enjoyment of the study of Western Civilization, increases your understanding of the ages you study, and helps you achieve high marks.

James T. Baker
Western Kentucky University

Study Guide

for Spielvogel's

WESTERN CIVILIZATION:

Fourth Edition

VOLUME II: Since 1550

14 DISCOVERY AND CRISIS IN THE SIXTEENTH AND SEVENTEENTH CENTURIES

Chapter Outline:

I.   An Age of Expansion and Discovery
    A.   The Motives Behind Them
        1.   A Long-time Fascination with the East
        2.   Hopes for Wealth through Trade
        3.   Christian Missions
        4.   The Technological Means Needed
    B.   The Portuguese Maritime Empire
        1.   Prince Henry, the Navigator
        2.   Bartholomew Diaz Around the Cape
        3.   Vasco da Gama to India
        4.   On to China
    C.   Voyages to the New World
        1.   Christopher Columbus
        2.   John Cabot
        3.   Ferdinand Magellan
        4.   The Treaty of Tordesillas
    D.   The Spanish Empire
        1.   Hernan Cortes and Mexico
        2.   Francisco Pizarro and Peru
        3.   Administration
            a.   *Encomienda*
            b.   *Audiencias*
    E.   The Impact of Expansion
        1.   Destruction of Native Cultures
        2.   The Enrichment of Europeans
        3.   National Rivalries
        4.   The Belief in European Superiority

II. Politics and Wars of Religion in the Sixteenth Century
   A. The French Wars of Religion (1562-1598)
      1. Catholics Against Huguenots
      2. The War of the Three Henries (1588-89)
      3. Henry IV's Conversion to Catholicism
   B. Philip II and Militant Catholicism
      1. "The Most Catholic King"
      2. Leader of the Holy League
      3. Protestant Revolt in the Spanish Netherlands
      4. William of Orange and Dutch Independence
   C. The England of Elizabeth
      1. The Act of Supremacy
      2. Mary Queen of Scots
      3. The Spanish Armada

III. Economic and Social Crises
   A. Inflation followed by Stagnation
   B. Trade, Industry, Banking, and Agriculture
   C. Population and the Growth of Cities

IV. Seventeenth-Century Crises: War and Rebellions
   A. The Thirty Years' War (1618-1648)
      1. Religious Motivations
      2. Controversy over "German Liberties"
      3. The Bohemian Phase
      4. The Danish Phase
      5. The Swedish Phase
      6. The Franco-Swedish Phase
      7. Peace of Westphalia
   B. A Military Revolution?
      1. Greater Firepower
      2. Flexibility and Mobility
      3. Discipline
   C. Rebellions
      1. Peasant
      2. Noble

V. The Witchcraft Craze
   A. A Search for Scapegoats
   B. The *Malleus Maleficarum*
   C. Increases in Trials
   D. Witch Stereotypes

VI. Culture in a Turbulent World
  A. Art: Mannerism and Baroque
    1. El Greco
    2. Peter Paul Rubens
    3. Gian Lorenzo Bernini
  B. Thought: The World of Michel Montaigne
  C. A Golden Age of Literature
    1. England's William Shakespeare
    2. Spain's Lope de Vega and Miguel de Cervantes

Chapter Summary:

The energies released by the Renaissance and the rivalries unleashed by the Reformation made the late sixteenth and seventeenth centuries a time of discovery, expansion, political chaos, and intellectual growth. It was an age of danger, opportunity, and achievement.

Portuguese and then Spanish explorers sailed around Africa to India and the Far East and then across the Atlantic to discover the Americas. Soon there were European empires in far places, and soon all of the nations of Europe were competing for trade routes and foreign colonies.

The Reformation which had divided Europe into warring religious camps now brought battles between and even within nation-states over who held the true Christian faith. The French and Spanish Catholic power structures sought to enforce their religious views on subjects: in France a Protestant minority called Huguenots, in Spanish territories a Dutch Protestant minority. In England, where the Elizabethan age had confirmed the nation's Protestantism, Catholics were subject to the same treatment Protestants received from France and Spain. The Holy Roman Empire, however, saw the most protracted and violent of the Religious Wars, one that lasted for thirty years. In the midst of all this chaos, both Protestants and Catholics turned their frustrations and hostilities on people they accused of practicing witchcraft.

Yet despite the turbulence of the day, the world of art, philosophy, and literature moved toward Enlightenment. El Greco, Rubens, and Bernini gave visible expression to the dreams of a harsh age, while Montaigne constructed a new form of philosophical expression and both Shakespeare and Cervantes fashioned literary masterpieces that shaped modern literature. A difficult age, but a wonderful age as well.

Identify:

1. Henry the Navigator

2. Vasco da Gama

3. Columbus

4. *Encomienda*

5. *Casa de Contratacion*

6. Huguenots

7. Duke of Alva

8. William of Orange

9. Mary Queen of Scots

10. Armada

11. Gustavus Adolphus

12. *Malleus Maleficarum*

13. Mannerism

14. El Greco

15. Baroque

16. Peter Paul Rubens

17. Montaigne

18. Lord Chamberlain's Company

19. Lope de Vega

20. Cervantes

Match the Following Words with their Definitions:

1. Ferdinand Magellan

2. Treaty of Tordesillas

3. Francesco Pizarro

4. Pacification of Ghent

5. Peace of Westphalia

6. Jacob Sprenger

7. El Greco

8. Peter Paul Rubens

9. Gian-Lorenzo Bernini

10. Michel de Montaigne

A. Agreement between Dutch provinces to stand together against Spain

B. Baroque artist who celebrated the beauty of the nude human body

C. Agreement which divided non-Christian lands between Spain and Portugal

D. French lawyer who created the modern essay form

E. Spanish explorer whose expedition was the first to circumnavigate the earth

F. Painter whose work captured the religious tensions of the Reformation Era

G. Agreement that ended the Thirty Years' War

H. Author of the standard early modern book on witchcraft

I. Spanish general who conquered the Incan Empire

J. Baroque artist who completed the building of Saint Peter's Church

Choose the Correct Answer:

1. Portugal expansionism was motivated by

    a. Religious zeal to convert China
    b. A desire for profit in spices
    c. The strong will of members of the royal family
    d. All of the above

2. Spanish expansion and exploration of the New World was best characterized by

    a. The first circumnavigation of the globe by Amerigo Vespucci
    b. The conquest of the Aztec Empire by Cortes
    c. The conquest of the Incas by Magellan
    d. The discovery of California by Pizarro

3. The name America that was given to the New World came from Amerigo Vespucci, who was

    a. A Spanish pirate
    b. An Italian writer
    c. An Italian missionary
    d. A Portuguese governmental official

4. Hernando Cortes looked on Native Americans as

    a. Poor people who needed western goods and services
    b. A cultured people who could make Europe a better place
    c. A people to be conquered and exploited
    d. A possible threat to Spain's mastery of the seas

5. Bartholome de Las Casas, a Dominican monk, was known for his

    a. Cruel and barbarous treatment of the Indians
    b. Magnificent lifestyle in a Cuban monastery
    c. Championing the plight of Indians under Spanish rule
    d. Conversion to a heathen religion and founding of the Native American Catholic Church

6. The French religious minority, the Huguenots, were spiritual descendants of

    a. Thomas Aquinas
    b. Martin Luther
    c. Michel Montaigne
    d. John Calvin

7. The religious climate of France prior to the French Wars of Religion was best characterized by

    a. A nobility that was nearly 50% Huguenot
    b. A population split evenly between Huguenots and Catholics
    c. Catherine de Medici's complete suppression of Huguenots
    d. A poorly organized Huguenot opposition to a Catholic majority

8. The French Wars of Religion from 1562 to 1598

    a. Ended with Henry of Navarre's Edict of Nantes, which gave toleration both to Huguenots and Catholics
    b. Saw the Huguenots win on the battlefield and force the Catholics to recognize them
    c. Ended when the Saint Bartholomew's Day Massacre killed the last of the Huguenots
    d. Were entirely a French affair, without ties to conflicts elsewhere

9. Under Elizabeth Tudor, England

    a. Purged all Catholics and Puritans
    b. Saw Catholicism restored to power
    c. Suffered a humiliating defeat by the Spanish Armada
    d. Became the leader of Protestant Europe

10. The English military posture under Queen Elizabeth

    a. Was mainly covert, with aid to pirates and Huguenots
    b. Was extremely aggressive, provoking wars everywhere
    c. Was that of a weak and declining power, unable to influence world affairs
    d. Was symbolic of the queen's complete disinterest in affairs on the continent

11. The execution of Mary Queen of Scots led to

    a. An end to religious conflict in England
    b. The end of the Scottish monarchy
    C. A marriage contract for Elizabeth
    d. A Spanish attempt to invade England

12. Which of the following statements best applies to the economy of sixteenth and seventeenth-century Europe?

    a. The joint-stock trading company raised huge sums for world trading ventures
    b. There was a general stagnation in mining and other metallurgy
    c. Technological innovations improved the lives of the peasants dramatically
    d. Population growth made for larger and more democratic cities across the continent

13. The event that sparked the Thirty Years' War was

    a.   A Protestant noble rebellion against the Catholic Ferdinand of Bohemia
    b.   The invasion of France by Frederick IV
    c.   The Spanish conquest of the Netherlands and the Inquisition that followed
    d.   The overthrow of Spanish rule in the New World by the Dutch

14. The Thirty Years' War had four phases and included all of the following *except* a

    a.   Bohemian phase
    b.   Swedish phase
    c.   Dutch phase
    d.   Danish phase

15. As a result of the Thirty Years' War and the Peace of Westphalia in 1648

    a.   The German economy was totally destroyed
    b.   Each German state could choose its own religion, with the exception of Calvinism
    c.   The growing gulf between religious and political motives became clear
    d.   The Holy Roman Empire was made secure for another hundred years

16. During the seventeenth century peasant revolts occurred in

    a.   France
    h   Hungary
    c.   Russia
    d.   All of the above

17. The witchhunts of the sixteenth and seventeenth centuries

    a.   Grew out of social unrest due to the shift from communalism to individualism
    b.   Were directed at the wealthy by their jealous neighbors
    c.   Were in no way sanctioned by organized religious groups
    d.   Were restricted to rural areas

18. Witchcraft hysteria declined in part because

    a.   Women organized for self defense
    b.   Destruction brought by the religious wars made people more tolerant
    c.   A papal decree condemned violence against misfits
    d.   Covens were all destroyed

19. Which of the following is the correct description?

    a.   Rubens—French dramatist
    b.   Cervantes—Mannerist painter
    c.   Shakespeare—the first novelist
    d.   Montaigne—creator of the essay form

20. The late 1500s and early 1600s were a time of

    a.   Great accomplishments in English theater
    b.   Dramatic decline in theater everywhere in Europe
    c.   New directions in Latin literature
    d.   A return to the morality plays of the Middle Ages

Complete the Following Sentences:

1. Encouraged by the support of Prince Henry, known as the _____, Portuguese sailor _____ _____ _____ found a sea
route to India, where Alfonso _____ set up the beginnings of an empire.

2. In the Americas, Spaniard _____ _____ conquered the
Aztecs, while _____ _____ conquered the Incas, setting
off a slaughter condemned by the monk Bartolome _____ _____
_____.

3. Religious turmoil in France erupted into violence in 1572 when 3,000 _____
were murdered on _____ _____ Day, a massacre
inspired by the _____ family.

4. In 1559 the English parliament passed a new Act of _____, making
_____ both spiritual and temporal ruler, ending the Catholic policies of her
sister _____.

5. In 1588 Philip II sent an _____ to invade England and restore the
_____ church, but it was battered by storms off the coasts of
_____ and _____.

6. The Thirty Years War, considered the last of the _____ wars, began with a
dispute in _____ and ended with the Peace of _____.

7. Domenikos Theotocopoulos, known to the world of art as _____ _____,
    brought _____ to its highest level while working in the Spanish city
    _____.

8. In his famous sculpture of Saint _____, Bernini sought to portray the
    _____ experience but also demonstrated physical _____.

9. Michel de Montaigne was so disgusted by _____ warfare that he left his
    career as a _____ to write essays whose aim was to _____
    _____.

10. Shakespeare came to London in the reign of _____ and wrote plays for his
    _____ _____ Company, which performed in such theaters
    as the _____ and the _____.

Place the Following in Chronological Order and Give Dates:

1. Edict of Nantes   1.

2. Montaigne's *Essays* published   2.

3. Battle of Lepanto   3.

4. Saint Bartholomew's Day Massacre   4.

5. Defeat of the Spanish Armada   5.

6. Peace of Westphalia   6.

7. Death of Elizabeth I   7.

Questions for Critical Thought:

1. What were the most important factors leading to Europe's expansion in the sixteenth century?

2. Describe the empire which the Spanish established in the Americas: its government, its social
    and religious systems, its economy, its strengths and weaknesses.

3. Discuss the impact the age of discovery and expansion abroad had on European society at home.

4. In recounting the French religious wars, what peculiarly "French" characteristics do you find in them? What events in French history had helped create these characteristics?

5. What personality traits, decisions, and policies caused Spain's Philip II to be a royal failure?

6. Describe the Elizabethan religious settlement in England. Was the Church of England Protestant or Catholic? Why did it work so well?

7. Discuss the causes, major periods, and consequences for European society of the Thirty Years' War.

8. Explain the witch hunt craze of the seventeenth century. What conditions fueled it, and why did it at long last end?

9. Compare the lives and achievements of Montaigne, Shakespeare, and Cervantes. What do these men's careers tell you about each one's country in the sixteenth and seventeenth centuries?

Analysis of Primary Source Documents:

1. What did Cortes think of the Aztec civilization he conquered? What does he indicate made him feel justified in destroying it? What does this say about his own Spanish civilization?

2. Try to separate fact from fiction in Las Casas' account of the treatment of Native Americans by Spanish conquistadors. Is there enough fact and is it serious enough to cause a conscientious Spanish official to order changes? If so, how would you suggest he start?

3. What do the two passages you have read tell you about Philip II? List other kinds of documents you would need before you could write a brief biography of the man.

4. How does Queen Elizabeth's speech before Parliament in 1601 demonstrate her political acumen? To what extent did her status as an unmarried woman add to the image she adopted as her public *persona*?

5. Describe the treatment of peasants on the farm captured by foreign soldiers during the Thirty Years' War, as recounted in the novel *Simplicius Simplicissimus*. To what extent do you see exaggeration for effect, and to what extent does this account agree with what you have read of treatment of civilians in other wars?

6.   From the witchcraft case you have read, what "rules" of law did the witch hunters of the seventeenth century follow? How would a modern defense attorney attack their case?

7.   How much of Shakespeare's tribute to England in "Richard II" is patriotism, how much xenophobia, and how much the dramatist's wish to please his audience? Give examples of your opinion.

Map Exercise 9: European Overseas Possessions in 1658

Using various shades of pencil, color and label the following:

1. Brazil
2. Canton
3. Caribbean Sea
4. India
5. Indian Ocean
6. Indonesia
7. Mozambique
8. New Spain
9. Peru
10. Philippines

Pinpoint and label the following:

1. Calicut
2. Cape of Good Hope
3. Ceylon
4. Goa
5. Hispaniola
6. Macao
7. Tenochtitlan
8. Zanzibar

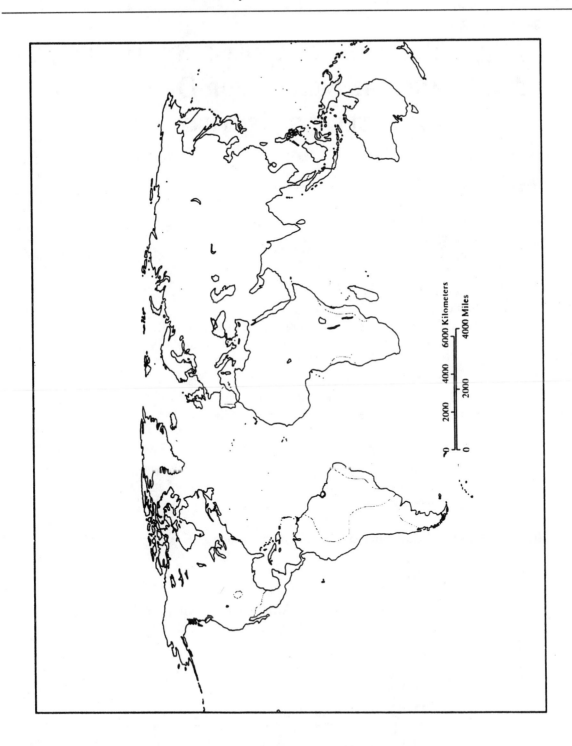

15 RESPONSE TO CRISIS: STATE BUILDING AND THE SEARCH FOR ORDER IN THE SEVENTEENTH CENTURY

Chapter Outline:

I. The Theory of Absolutism
    A. By Jean Bodin
    B. By Jacques Bossuet

II. Absolutism in Modern Europe
    A. France's Absolute Monarchy
        1. Cardinal Richelieu's Centralization of Power under Louis XIII
        2. Cardinal Mazarin during the Minority of Louis XIV
        3. The Reign of Louis XIV (1643-1715)
            a. "The Sun King"
            b. Control of State and Church
            c. Finances and the Court at Versailles
            d. Louis' Wars
    B. The Decline of Spain
        1. Expulsion of the Moriscos
        2. Reforms by Guzman
        3. Wars and Taxes

III. Absolutism in Central, Eastern, and Northern Europe
    A. The German States
        1. Brandenburg-Prussia
            a. The House of Hohenzollern
            b. Frederick William's Army and his Commissariat
            c. Elector Frederick III Becomes King Frederick I

        2.   The Emergence of Austria
            a.   The House of Habsburg
            b.   Leopold I's Move to the East
            c.   A Multiculture Empire
- **B.**   Italy: From Spanish to Austrian Rule
- **C.**   Muscovy Becomes Russia
        1.   The Reign of Ivan the Terrible
        2.   The Reign of Peter (the Great) Romanov (1689-1725)
            a.   Centralization of Authority
            b.   Westernization
            c.   Peter's Wars
- **D.**   The Growth of Monarchy in Scandinavia
        1.   Denmark
        2.   Sweden
- **E.**   The Ottoman Empire
        1.   The Victories of Suleiman I
        2.   A European State
- **F.**   The Limits of Absolutism

IV.   Limited Monarchies and Republics
- **A.**   The Weakness of the Polish Monarchy
        1.   An Elective System
        2.   A Confederation of Estates
- **B.**   The "Golden Age" of the Dutch Republic
        1.   Independence following the Peace of Westphalia
        2.   Religious Tolerance
        3.   Economic Prosperity
        4.   Amsterdam as a Commercial Capital
- **C.**   England and the Emergence of Constitutional Monarchy
        1.   Charles I and Civil War
        2.   Oliver Cromwell and the Commonwealth
        3.   The Stuart Restoration and Charles II
        4.   James II and the "Glorious Revolution"
        5.   William and Mary and the Bill of Rights
        6.   Responses to the English Revolution
            a.   Thomas Hobbes and *Leviathan*
            b.   John Locke and the Right of Revolution

V.   Economic Trends
- **A.**   Mercantilism: State Regulation of the Economy

    B.   Overseas Trade and Colonies
        1.   The Decline of Portugal and Spain
        2.   The Rise of the Dutch and English

VI.   The World of Seventeenth-Century Culture
    A.   Art: French Classicism and Dutch Realism
        1.   Nicholas Poussin
        2.   Rembrandt van Rijn
    B.   The Theater: The Triumph of French Neoclassicism
        1.   Jean-Baptise Racine's Greek Tragedies
        2.   Jean-Baptiste Moliere's Satires

Chapter Summary:

The political and religious crises of the Sixteenth and early Seveneenth Centuries led philosophers and rulers to consider alternatives to what they considered the insecure and often chaotic institutional structures of the day. For over a century both groups defended the growth of power at the top, strong monarchies that could keep the peace and order, who could enforce social uniformity, who could take measures to increase national prosperity.

Government moved increasingly toward absolutism, toward kings stronger than any known in Europe before, kings with power to provide order and prosperity. While absolutism reached its apex in France with the reign of Louis XIV, it had significant successes in Spain, the German states, Italy, Russia, and the Ottoman Empire. Everywhere there was a movement toward centralized power, the weakening of local rulers, and state control of economies.

Only in a few nations did royal power diminish and begin to share rule with parliamentary and constitutional systems. It did happen in Poland, in the United Provinces of Holland, and most importantly in Britain. In the latter there occurred in 1688 a bloodless revolution against James II, whom Parliament replaced with the dual monarchy of William and Mary, who promised certain rights to British citizens. There the way was paved not only for limited monarchy but also for democracy.

This Age of Absolutism was an age of cultural and philosophical achievement. It was the Golden Age of Dutch painting, exemplified by the work of Rembrandt. It was an age when the French theater gained world dominance, as demonstrated by the work of Moliere and Racine. It was a time of ferment in political theory: the absolutist conjectures of Thomas Hobbes; the social contract of John Locke. In many ways the Enlightenment was beginning.

Identify:

1.   Absolutism

2.   Richelieu

3.   Sun King

4.   Le Tellier

5.   Colbert

6.   War of the Spanish Succession

7.   Gibraltar

8.   Gaspar de Guzman

9.   Hohenzollerns

10.   Habsburgs

11.   Ivan the Terrible

12.   Michael Romanov

13.   Great Northern War

14.   St. Petersburg

15.   Glorious Revolution

16.   Toleration Act

17.   *Leviathan*

18.   Mercantilism

19.   Rembrandt

20.   Moliere

Match the Following Words with their Definitions:

1. Mazarin

2. Fronde

3. Versailles

4. Oliver Cromwell

5. Bill of Rights

6. Thomas Hobbes

7. John Locke

8. Mercantilism

9. Nicholas Poussin

10. Jean-Baptist Racine

A. Argued that if a monarch broke his social contract, the people had the right to form a new government

B. Granted Parliament the right to levy taxes

C. Leader of the British Commonwealth

D. Belief that a nation's wealth depends on its gold and silver reserves

E. He argued that order demanded absolute monarchy

F. Playwright who pursued classical themes

G. Center of Louis XIV's royal government

H. A rebellion of the French nobility against the royal family

I. His paintings illustrate the principles of the French Academy

J. He dominated the French government when Louis XIV was a child

Choose the Correct Answer:

1. One result of the Seventeenth Century crises in Europe was

    a. An increased role of the church in secular society
    b. A trend toward democratic reforms in government
    c. The division of empires into smaller feudal kingdoms
    d. A trend toward absolutism, as exemplified by Louis XIV

2.   As Louis XIII's chief minister, Cardinal Richelieu was most successful in

    a.   Evicting the Huguenots from France
    b.   Strengthening the central role of the monarchy
    c.   Creating a reservoir of funds for the treasury
    d.   Emerging victorious in the Fronde revolts

3.   The series of noble revolts known as the Fronde resulted in

    a.   The assassination in 1661 of Cardinal Mazarin
    b.   Increased power for the Parlement of Paris
    c.   A stronger, more secure, more unified noble army
    d.   Frenchmen looking to the monarchy for stability

4.   Louis XIV was most successful in controlling the administration of his kingdom by

    a.   Working closely with hereditary, aristocratic officeholders
    b.   Using his intendants as direct royal agents
    c.   Employing royal patronage to "bribe" officers to execute the king's policies
    d.   Eliminating town councils and legislative bodies in the provinces

5.   Louis XIV restructured the policy-making machinery of the French government by

    a.   Personally dominating the actions of his ministers and secretaries
    b.   Stacking the royal council with high nobles and royal princes
    c.   Selecting his ministers from established aristocratic families
    d.   All of the above

6.   Louis XIV's military adventures resulted in

    a.   French domination of Western Europe
    b.   Defeat after defeat by coalitions of nations
    c.   The union of the thrones of France and Spain
    d.   Increased popular support of Louis in France

7.   Activities at the court of Versailles included all of the following *except*

    a.   Gambling with large sums of money
    b.   The humiliation of noble courtiers
    c.   Successful challenges to Louis' authority
    d.   An overwhelming concern with etiquette

8.   The overall practical purpose of the Versailles system was

       a.   To exclude the high nobility from real power
       b.   To serve as a hospital for Louis when he was ill
       c.   To act as a reception hall for foreign visitors
       d.   To give Louis a life of absolute privacy

9.   The trend in Spain during the Seventeenth Century was

       a.   Economic growth because of New World colonies
       b.   The loss of European possessions
       c.   A waning in the power of the Catholic church
       d.   The emergence of a dominant middle class

10.   The "Time of Troubles" describes

       a.   An anarchic period in Russian history before the rise of the Romanov dynasty
       b.   A time of religious turmoil in which Old Believer Russians committed suicide
       c.   A period of revolt led by Cossack Stenka Razin
       d.   A part of the reign of Tsar Alexis, who made serfdom legal in Russia

11.   The cultural reforms of Peter the Great

       a.   Failed to change habits of dress and grooming
       b.   Left the Orthodox Church untouched
       c.   Required Russian men to wear beards
       d.   Permitted Russian women many new freedoms

12.   In his efforts to Europeanize Russia, Peter the Great

       a.   Used conscription to build a standing army of 30,000 men
       b.   Reorganized the government so that the Duma and consultative bodies played a
              dominant role
       c.   Adopted mercantilistic policies to stimulate growth of the economy
       d.   Built a "police state" with the aid of aristocratic bureaucrats

13.   Peter the Great's primary foreign policy goal was

       a.   To open a warm-water port accessible to Europe for Russia
       b.   The utter destruction of the Ottoman Empire
       c.   Victory and control over the Scandinavian countries
       d.   The conquest of Germany

14. The most successful of the absolute rulers of the Seventeenth Century were those who

     a. Used older systems of administration to their advantage
     b. Crushed the power of the landed aristocracy
     c. Dominated the lives of their subjects at every level
     d. All of the above

15. Between 1688 and 1832, Britain's government was in fact, if not in name

     a. A plutocracy
     b. An oligarchy
     c. A theocracy
     d. An absolute monarchy

16. The British Declaration of Rights and Bill of Rights

     a. Laid the foundation for a constitutional monarchy
     b. Resolved England's seventeenth-century religious feuds
     c. Reaffirmed the divine-right theory of kingship
     d. Gave the king the right to raise armies without consent of Parliament

17. Thomas Hobbes' "Leviathan" was a

     a. Snake that killed a little Dutch boy
     h   Mythical Frankish king, a role model for James II
     c. State with the power to keep order
     d. Principle of the right to revolution

18. The seventeenth-century political theorist closest to the thinking of Eighteenth Century
     American colonists was

     a. Thomas Hobbes
     b. Hugo Grotius
     c. John Locke
     d. Michael Klembara

19. The flowering of Seventeenth Century culture witnessed all of the following *except*

    a. France replacing Italy as Europe's cultural center
    b. The French neoclassical theater's break with royal patronage, as demonstrated by Moliere's plays
    c. A Golden Age in Dutch painting, exemplified by Rembrandt
    d. The neoclassical emphasis on the clever and polished over the emotional and imaginative

20. The mercantilist policies that dominated Europe's economy in the Seventeenth Century

    a. Concerned itself with the changing volume of trade
    b. Stressed co-prosperity among nations through fair trading practices
    c. Were responsible for great economic and population growth through the century
    d. Focused on the role of the state in the successful conduct of economic affairs

Complete the Following Sentences:

1. Henry IV granted French Huguenots civil rights with his Edict of _____, but Louis XIV took them away with his Edict _____ _____.

2. Jean-Baptiste Colbert, controller-general of _____ for Louis XIV, followed the policy of _____, encouraging _____, discouraging _____.

3. The suspicion that France and Spain would be united grew strong when Louis XIV's _____ became Philip V, leading to the War of the _____ _____.

4. The Hohenzollern ruler who built Prussia was the Great Elector _____ _____, who based his strength on a large and efficient _____ and used a _____ to raise revenues.

5. In Italy, the three arms of the Counter-Reformation, the _____, the _____, and the _____, stifled all resistance to Catholic orthodoxy.

6. Peter Romanov, who was raised in Moscow's _____ _____, decided after a trip to _____ Europe that Russia was _____ and needed changes.

7.   When it became evident to the English that James II's baby son would perpetuate a
        _____ dynasty, a revolution exiled him in favor of William of
        _____ and his wife _____, daughter of James II.

8.   American and French used Englishman's John Locke's theories to demand
        _____ government, the rule of _____, and protection of
        _____.

9.   The Golden Age of Dutch painting was financed by the supremacy of Dutch
        _____ and reached its height with the work of _____.

10.   Moliere got away with satirizing court life in his play *The* _____, but he was
        in hot water when his *Tartuffe* made fun of the _____.

Place the Following in Chronological Order and Give Dates:

1.   Peter Romanov's trip to the West   1.

2.   War of the Spanish Succession   2.

3.   Turkish siege of Vienna   3.

4.   England's Glorious Revolution   4.

5.   Publication of Hobbes' *Leviathan*   5.

6.   Michael Romanov begins his reign   6.

7.   Edict of Fontainebleau   7.

Questions for Critical Thought:

1.   Outline the theory of Absolutism, and illustrate it, using France under Louis XIV as your
        example.

2.   List and explain the steps in Louis XIV's steady march toward absolute rule in France. What
        do you consider the most crucial steps for his eventual success?

3.   Describe in detail the life of the aristocracy at Louis XIV's court in Versailles. To what extent was Louis master and to what extent a slave of his court?

4.   What factors transformed the rather unpromising German province of Brandenburg-Prussia into the core of what was to be a German nation? Explain each factor.

5.   Describe Peter Romanov's role in the emergence of modern Russia. Was he more or less important for Russia than Louis XIV was for France? Explain your answer.

6.   Name several nations that became either limited monarchies or republics rather than absolute monarchies. In each case explain why it developed as it did—and did not.

7.   Explain what made the Dutch so commercially successful in the Seventeenth Century. Why did no other nation find such success? Give examples.

8.   Describe the way a near-absolute monarchy became the world's first truly constitutional monarchy in Britain. What three persons do you feel contributed most to this change, and why?

9.   List and explain the new political theories that grew out of the Age of Absolutism. Show how each one was a product of its time.

10.   Give a full definition of mercantilism, and demonstrate using the Dutch example how, in practice, it worked.

Analysis of Primary Source Documents:

1.   How do Louis XIV's *Memoirs* show that he had given some thought to the duties of a king? How well did his theory fit his actions?

2.   From Saint-Simon's account of Louis XIV's life, what do you really feel the king thought of women?

3.   Explain how Peter Romanov's treatment of the rebellious Streltsy might demonstrate Machiavelli's notion that the effective ruler must act without consideration for the usual principles of morality.

4.   Sum up in one sentence how, according to John Keymer, the Dutch were economically outstripping other nations in the Seventeenth Century. Then explain your statement with ample illustrations.

5.   Explain how the 1688 British Bill of Rights paved the way for constitutional government. Show how this Bill influenced American colonists in the next century.

6.   How do Thomas Hobbes and John Locke agree and disagree on political authority? What forms of government would each one's theories lead a society to adopt?

7.   What does King Louis' letter to the King of Tonkin tell you about his devotion to French tradition, and what does the reply tell you about the King of Tonkin's devotion to his own tradition?

8.   How did Moliere satirize the world of scholarship? To what extent do you think his audience would have taken his joke seriously?

Map Exercise 10: Europe in 1648

Using various shades of pencil, color and label the following:

1.   Baltic Sea
2.   Bavaria
3.   Bohemia
4.   Brandenburg
5.   British Isles
6.   Denmark
7.   Estonia
8.   Finland
9.   Hungary
10.   Kingdom of the Two Sicilies
11.   Norway
12.   Ottoman Empire
13.   Poland
14.   Portugal
15.   Prussia
16.   Russia
17.   Sweden
18.   Swiss Confederation
19.   Tuscany
20.   United Provinces

Pinpoint and label the following:

1.   Amsterdam
2.   Berlin
3.   Budapest
4.   Danzig
5.   Naples
6.   Paris
7.   Venice
8.   Vienna
9.   Warsaw

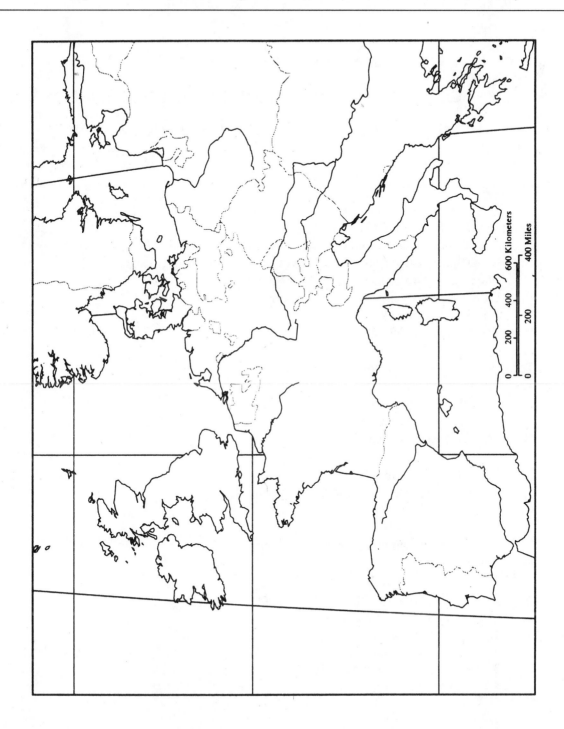

CHAPTER

16 Toward a New Heaven and a New Earth: The Scientific Revolution and the Emergence of Modern Science

Chapter Outline:

I. Background to the Scientific Revolution
    A. The Medieval Reliance on Classical Authority
    B. Renaissance Scholars and the Discovery of classical disagreements
    C. The Artists and Close Observation of Nature
    D. Early Modern Technological Innovations
    E. New Understandings of Mathematics
    F. The Influence of Hermetic Magic

II. Toward a New heaven: A Revolution in Astronomy
    A. The Ptolomaic Model
        1. Ptolemy and Aristotle
        2. A Geocentric Universe
    B. The Work of Copernicus
        1. *On the Revolutions of the Heavenly Spheres*
        2. The Heliocentric Model
        3. Early Christian Reactions to Copernicus
    C. The Role of Tycho Brahe
        1. Uraniborg Castle
        2. Detailed Observations
    D. Johannes Kepler
        1. The "Music of the Spheres"
        2. The Three Laws of Planetary Motion
    E. Galileo and Controversy
        1. Galileo's Telescope
        2. *The Starry Messenger*
        3. Trial Before the Inquisition
        4. Laws of Motion

F.   Isaac Newton and Universal Physics
1.   The *Principia*
2.   The Universal Law of Gravity

III.   Advances in Medicine
A.   The Influence of Galen
1.   Animal Dissection
2.   The "Four Humors"
B.   Paracelsus
1.   Medicine as Chemistry
2.   "Like Cures Like"
C.   Andreas Vesalius
1.   Human Dissection
2.   A Correction of Galen
D.   William Harvey and the Human Blood System

IV.   Women in the Origins of Modern Science
A.   Informal Educations and Exclusion from Universities
B.   Margaret Cavendish
1.   Critiques of Scientific Method and Theory
2.   An Inspiration to Other Women
C.   Maria Merian and Caterpillars
D.   Maria Winklemann
1.   Discovery of a Comet
2.   Rejection by the Berlin Academy
E.   The *Querelles des Femmes*
1.   The Male Agreement About Female Inferiority
2.   A Diminished Medical Role for Women

V.   Toward a New Earth: Descartes, Rationalism, and a New View of Humankind
A.   Descartes' *Discourse on Method*
1.   Rejection of the Senses
2.   Separation of Mind and Matter
B.   The Implications of Cartesian Dualism

VI.   The Scientific Method
A.   Francis Bacon
1.   His *Great Instauration*
2.   The Inductive Method
3.   A Practical Science
B.   Rene Descartes' Emphasis on Deduction and Mathematics
C.   Isaac Newton's Synthesis of Bacon and Descartes

VII. Science and Religion in the Seventeenth Century
    A. The Example of Galileo
        1. A Split Between Science and Religion
        2. Attempts at a New Synthesis
    B. Benedict de Spinoza
        1. Excommunciation from the Amsterdam Synagogue
        2. Panentheism
        3. A Philosophy of Reason
    C. Blaise Pascal
        1. His *Pensées*: An Apology for the Christian Faith
        2. The Limits of Science and Reason

VIII. The Spread of Scientific Knowledge
    A. Scientific Societies
        1. The Royal Society of England
        2. The Royal Academy of France
        3. Scientific Journals
    B. Science and Society
        1. Acceptance through Practicality
        2. Science As a Means of Economic Progress and Social Stability

Chapter Summary:

At the same time that kings were consolidating power and seeking a new social order based on absolute rule, an intellectual revolution was taking place which would change educated people's understanding of the universe, of man's nature, and even the nature of truth itself. This revolution in science provided new models both for heaven and for earth.

The Scientific Revolution began with astronomy, and conclusions drawn by mathematicians and observers like Copernicus, Kepler, Galileo, and Newton both provided new understandings of the universe and its laws and called into question the wisdom of ancient and medieval scholars. From the study of astronomy and the realization that by empirical observation one can know the truth about the universe, various scholars, male and female, began questioning and revising opinions about medicine and the human sciences.

Parallel to the revolution in imperial studies was a new emphasis on human reason. Started by Rene Descartes and his famous *Discourse on Method*, the new claims for rationalism focused attention on the nature and capacities of mankind. While empiricism and rationalism were at times in conflict, they eventually merged to create a scholarship that rejected both tradition and authority in favor of continual reevaluation of established knowledge.

Religious sensitivities were ruffled by these secular endeavors, and scientists often found themselves at odds with religious powers. Even some of the scientists themselves were disturbed by the results of their studies. Pascal dedicated his life to the reconciliation of science and religion, but his life was too brief to develop all of his ideas fully.

Yet science was too careful about its conclusions to be discredited and proved itself too useful to the world to be silenced. Scientific societies, sponsored by kings, began disseminating discoveries, and the general public began benefitting from what the scientists were doing. The modern world of progress and doubt was on its way.

Identify:

1.   Hermetic

2.   Geocentric

3.   Heliocentric

4.   Music of the Spheres

5.   Simplicio

6.   *Principia*

7.   Paracelsus

8.   Vesalius

9.   Harvey

10.   Margaret Cavendish

11.   Maria Merian

12.   *Querelles des femmes*

13.   Jean de La Bruyere

14.   Cartesian dualism

15.   Spinoza

16.   Pascal

17. Royal Society

18. Royal Academy

19. *Journal des Savants*

20. *Philosophical Transactions*

Match the Following Words with their Definitions:

1. Nicholas Copernicus

2. Tycho Brahe

3. Johannes Kepler

4. *The Starry Messenger*

5. Isaac Newton

6. William Harvey

7. Maria Winkelmann

8. Rene Descartes

9. *Pensées*

10. Royal Academy of Sciences

A. He advocated a geometric universe and tried to discover the "music of the spheres"

B. He discovered the circulation of blood and showed it was caused by the pumping of the heart

C. As astronomer denied a post in the Berlin Academy

D. He made astronomical observations from an island given him by the King of Denmark

E. An attempt to reconcile science and religion

F. Colbert's contribution to the French scientific revolution

G. President of the Royal Society and only scientist buried in Westminster Abbey

H. Through mathematical calculations came to regard Ptolomey's geocentric universe as too complicated

I. Advocate of rationalism who began his method with doubt of all things

J. Defense of Copernicus' system

Choose the Correct Answer:

1.   The Scientific Revolution of the Seventeenth Century was

      a.   Stimulated by a new interest in Galen and Aristotle
      b.   A direct result of the revolt against social conditions in the Middle Ages
      c.   Born in the new intellectual monasteries
      d.   More a gradual building on the accomplishments of previous centuries than a sudden
            shift in thought

2.   The greatest achievements in science during the Sixteenth and Seveneenth Centuries came in
      which three areas?

      a.   Astronomy, mechanics, and medicine
      b.   Astronomy, biology, and chemistry
      c.   Biology, mechanics, and ballistics
      d.   Engineering, physics, and dentistry

3.   The general conception of the universe before Copernicus held that

      a.   Heaven was at the center and the earth circled it
      b.   The earth was at a stationary center, while perfect crystalline spheres orbited it
      c.   The earth rested on the shell of a giant turtle
      d.   It was all a mystery known only to theologians

4.   Although he made statements about the construction of the universe, Copernicus was by
      formal training a

      a.   Mathematician
      b.   Banker
      c.   Cloistered monk
      d.   Lawyer

5.   The universal theories proposed by Copernicus

      a.   Led to his arrest and imprisonment in a monastery
      b.   Were supported by Protestants in order to make the Catholics look foolish
      c.   Made the universe less complicated by rejecting Ptolemy's epicycles
      d.   Explained the appearance of the sun's rotation with a theory of earthly rotation

6.   Johannes Kepler believed that the truth of the universe could be found by combining the study of mathematics with that of

    a.   Neoplatonic magic
    b.   Greek literature
    c.   The Book of Revelation
    d.   Shakespearean tragedy

7.   Galileo held that the planets were

    a.   Composed of material much like that of earth
    b.   Reflections of the divine city
    c.   Spheres composed of pure energy
    d.   Merely mirages in the "desert" of space

8.   Isaac Newton's scientific discoveries

    a.   Were met with more hostility in England than on the continent of Europe
    b.   Formed the basis for universal physics until well into the Twentieth Century
    c.   Completely divorced God from the universe and its laws
    d.   Were the first to be printed in a language other than Latin

9.   Newton's universal law of gravity

    a.   Offered an explanation for all motion in the universe
    b.   Had little practical application to the questions of universal motion
    c.   Showed that humans could never understand why God made things the way they are
    d.   Seemed to indicate that the universe began with a "big bang"

10.   Paracelsus revolutionized the world of medicine in the Sixteenth Century by

    a.   Disproving Galen's theory of two blood systems
    b.   Dissecting human rather than animal cadavers
    c.   Curing diseases with his "like cures like" philosophy
    d.   Rejecting "Christian Chemistry" as taught in the universities of his day

11.   The role of women in the Scientific Revolution was best characterized by

    a.   The way scientific communities welcomed women as members
    b.   Maria Merian's breakthrough in astronomy
    c.   The manner in which Margaret Cavendish debated science with men
    d.   Maria Winkelmann's professorship in physics at the University of Berlin

12.   The overall effect of the Scientific Revolution on the *querelles des femmes* arguments was to

   a.   Dispel old myths about female inferiority
   b.   Increase the role of husbands in child birth
   c.   Justify male dominance
   d.   Demonstrate that there was no inherent skeletal differences between the sexes

13.   Maria Merian contributed to the world of science—among other things—her remarkable illustrations of

   a.   Butterflies
   b.   Cats
   c.   Worms
   d.   Caterpillars

14.   Francis Bacon was important to the Scientific Revolution because of his emphasis on

   a.   Empirical, experimental observation
   b.   Pure, theoretical reasoning
   c.   Deductive conclusions, which moved from general to particular principles
   d.   The need for scientists to preserve nature

15.   Spinoza said that our failure to understand the true nature of God leads to

   a.   A false worship of nature
   b.   A society in which men use nature for selfish purposes
   c.   A decline in the powers of moral judgment
   d.   Sexual permissiveness

16.   Blaise Pascal believed that human beings

   a.   Can know God through pure reason
   b.   Are the summation of all things
   c.   Can understand only what is revealed to them in the Bible
   d.   Cannot understand infinity because only God can

17.   Organized religion in the Seventeenth Century

    a.   Conceded that only science can explain the universe
    b.   Rejected scientific discoveries that conflicted with Christian theology's view of the universe
    c.   Cooperated as an equal and willing partner to the study of science
    d.   Simply ignored science, calling it a new "toy for the minds of God's children"

18.   During the Seventeenth Century, royal and princely patronage of science

    a.   Declined
    b.   Continued only in Italy
    c.   Became an international phenomenon
    d.   Replaced church funding

19.   The new scientific societies established the first

    a.   Fundraising events for medical research
    b.   Journals describing discoveries
    c.   Codes of ethics for the treatment of animals
    d.   Endowed chairs of science in the universities

20.   Science became an integral part of Western culture in the Eighteenth Century because

    a.   People came to see it as the only way to find the truth
    b.   Its mechanistic theories were popular with kings
    c.   Radical groups like the Levellers, when they came to power, insisted on the supremacy of science
    d.   It offered a new means of making profit and maintaining social order

Complete the Following Sentences:

1.   Renaissance humanists demonstrated that not all ancient scholars agreed with
    _____ and _____, who were unquestioned in medieval science.

2.   Leonardo da Vinci reasoned that since God eternally _____, nature is inherently
    _____; yet at the same time scientists sought secrets of the universe through
    _____ magic.

3.   Copernicus rejected Ptolemy's _____ universe and postulated a
      _____ one because he found Ptolemy's system too _____.

4.   Peering through his telescope, Galileo discovered _____ on the moon, Jupiter's
      four _____, and _____ spots.

5.   Galileo explained the three approaches people might take to the new astronomy in his
      Dialogue, where three characters, _____, _____, and
      _____ argued the theory of Copernicus.

6.   During eighteen months back in his home villages from Cambridge, Isaac Newton invented
      _____, studied the composition of _____, and began work on the
      universal law of _____.

7.   Vesalius disputed Galen's assertion that blood vessels originate in the _____but did
      not doubt his claim that two different kinds of blood flow through the
      _____ and _____.

8.   Descartes argued that the _____ of man cannot be doubted but that the
      _____ _____ can be, thus creating what we call Cartesian
      _____.

9.   Thrown out of his Amsterdam _____ for heresy, Spinoza was a
      _____, not the atheist his critics claimed, believing that all things are in

10.   The Royal Society was chartered in 1662 by _____, while the Royal Academy of
      Sciences was recognized in 1666 by _____. Both emphasized the
      _____ value of scientific research.

Place the Following in Chronological Order and Give Dates:

1.	Harvey's *On the Motion of the Heart and Blood*	1.	
2.	Newton's *Principia*	2.	
3.	Copernicus' *On the Revolutions of the Heavenly Spheres*	3.	
4.	Bacon's *The Great Instauration*	4.	
5.	Descartes' *Discourse on Method*	5.	
6.	Pascal's *Pensées*	6.	
7.	Galileo's *The Starry Messenger*	7.	

Questions for Critical Thought:

1. Discuss the causes of the Scientific Revolution of the Seventeenth Century. Of these causes, which seems the strangest to modern minds? Why?

2. What did the new discoveries in Seventeenth Century astronomy contribute to the Scientific Revolution? What did each of the major astronomers add to the field?

3. Name the three men who added new knowledge to the field of medicine during the Seventeenth Century, and briefly describe each one's contribution to the field.

4. List the women who contributed to the Scientific Revolution, and briefly describe each one's contribution. Why did male scientists have such difficulties accepting them as equals?

5. Discuss the ways in which all of the new scientific discoveries affected the Seventeenth Century's image of man. How did the new image differ from the old one?

6. Describe the "scientific method," showing how you might use it to study a particular problem or question in a certain branch of science.

7.   How did the Scientific Revolution affect religious thought? How did religious thought affect the Revolution?

Analysis of Primary Source Documents:

1.   Using the *Life* of Jerome Cardan as your example, demonstrate the close relationship, as late as the Sixteenth Century, between science and what scientists would much later call superstition.

2.   Explain why Copernicus' heliocentric theory was at the same time so simple and so profound.

3.   Describe the "tone" of the famous correspondence between Kepler and Galileo. How can you explain the absence of apparent jealousy usually associated with famous men?

4.   What personality traits can you find in Galileo's account of his astronomical observations that would explain why he was a successful scientist?

5.   Show how Isaac Newtons' four rules of reasoning are the end result of two centuries in which the "scientific method" was developed and refined.

6.   Speculate on why—amid the scientific progress of his century and despite evidence to the contrary—Spinoza was so unprepared to accept women as equals.

7.   To what degree do you find Descartes' method for finding truth a good guide? Point out any difficulties one might meet applying it to Twentieth Century scientific problems.

8.   What was at the root of Pascal's doubts about man's ability to find scientific certainty? What problems for science of the future did he accurately pose?

17 THE EIGHTEENTH CENTURY: AN AGE OF ENLIGHTENMENT

Chapter Outline:

I. The Enlightenment
    A. "Dare to Know"
        1. Finding the Laws that Govern Human Society
        2. Using Them to Create a Better World
    B. The Paths to the Enlightenment
        1. Popular Understanding and Acceptance of Science
        2. A New Skepticism of Religion and Tradition
        3. Broader Travel and Literature that Disseminated Knowledge Gained Thereby
        4. John Locke's Theory of Knowledge
        5. Isaac Newton's Laws of Physics
    C. The Philosophes and Their Ideas
        1. Montesquieu's Critique of Society and Government
        2. Voltaire's Critique of Justice and Religion
        3. Diderot's *Encyclopedia* and a New Way of Thinking
    D. Toward a New "Science of Man"
        1. David Hume and the Birth of the New Human Science
        2. Quesnay and Laws Governing the Economy
        3. Adam Smith and a Study of *The Wealth of Nations*
    E. The Later Enlightenment
        1. Condorcet and the Nine Stages of History
        2. Jean-Jacques Rousseau and *The Social Contract*
    F. The "Woman's Question" in the Enlightenment
        1. Mary Astell and Sexual Equality
        2. Mary Wollstonecraft and Feminism
    G. The Social Environment of the Philosophes
        1. The Salon
        2. Secret Societies

Chapter Summary:

Each age builds upon the foundations of its predecessor, and never was this the case to a greater degree than the way the Eighteenth Century built upon the seventeenth. The revolution in science led directly to the Enlightenment and its revolution in philosophy.

The popularization of science, the growth of a healthy skepticism about tradition, the writings of world travelers, and the legacy of thinkers like John Locke and Isaac Newton brought about an Eighteenth Century flowering of philosophy which is considered one of the high points of Western civilization. The philosophes, Montesquieu, Voltaire, Diderot, Adam Smith, and Rousseau, left a body of thought and writing that is unsurpassed in the history of social criticism.

It was also an age of innovation in the arts. Rococo painting and architecture, classical music, and the birth of the novel form in literature all added style and color to the age. In the social sciences various writers began critically commenting on education, crime and punishment, and the social and economic causes behind historical events. The stage was set for modern scholarship and social criticism.

Christianity, which the philosophes blamed for many human woes, found itself in a hostile environment, with the institutional church branded archaic and intellectuals leaving it for what they considered a more respectable deism. Yet among the common people the traditional faith continued to have strong appeal and tenacity. A new era of piety swept both Protestant and Catholic camps; and England particularly experienced a new phenomenon, the popular revival meetings of the Wesleys.

The Enlightenment of the Eighteenth Century was the product of a revolution in science; and the ideas it so freely disseminated helped usher in the age of political revolution to come. It was both the child and the parent of revolution.

Identify:

1.   Enlightenment

2.   Montesquieu

3.   Denis Diderot

4.   David Hume

5.   Social Contract

6.   *Emile*

7.   Rococo

8.   Giovanni Battista Tiepolo

9.   Franz Joseph Haydn

10.   Henry Fielding

11.   *Spectator*

12.   Dissenting Academies

13.   Cesare Beccaria

14. Carnival

15. Almanac

16. Hannah More

17. Joseph II

18. "Jewish Problem"

19. Moravian Brethren

20. Methodism

Match the Following Words with their Definitions:

1.	Jean Calas	A.	Creator of the Baroque *St. Matthew's Passion*
2.	Deism	B.	Leading character in Henry Fielding's novel
3.	*Emile*	C.	Early magazine published by Addison and Steele
4.	Balthasar Neumann	D.	Belief in god the Creator without reference to Christian dogma
5.	J. S. Bach		
6.	W. A. Mozart	E.	Protestant defended by Voltaire when falsely accused of murder
7.	Tom Jones	F.	Banned from France in 1764
8.	*Spectator*	G.	Rococo architect who built the Wurzburg Residenz
9.	Jesuit	H.	Form of Protestant mysticism that emphasized good works
10.	Pietism	I.	Rousseau's imaginary student in his book on education
		J.	Prodigy who wrote *The Marriage of Figaro*

Choose the Correct Answer:

1. Bernard de Fontenelle, popularizer of scientific learning, was for fifty years secretary of the

   a. Royal Academy of Science
   b. National Library of France
   c. Royal Society of Surgeons
   d. Jesuit Order in France

2. The Enlightenment of the Eighteenth Century was characterized by the philosophes'

   a. Naive optimism that they could change society
   b. Rejection of traditional Christian dogma
   c. Emphasis on mysticism rather than rationalism
   d. Revival of medieval Scholasticism

3. The French philosophes

   a. Fashioned a grand, rational system of thought
   b. Flourished in an atmosphere of government support
   c. Called for the state to suppress ideas contrary to their own
   d. Left families behind to live in communes

4. In his *Spirit of the Laws*, Montesquieu was above all concerned with

   a. Supporting a strong monarchy
   b. Supporting a dominant legislature
   c. Elevating the judiciary to absolute power
   d. Maintaining a balance between the three branches

5. The pholosophical religion Deism was based on

   a. A Newtonian view of the world as a machine created by God
   b. A personal faith in God the loving father of Christ
   c. A vivid atheism
   d. A strong patriotism in which the state is the new church

6.   Voltaire was perhaps best known for his criticism of

   a.   The German state and its militarism
   b.   The modern idea of separation of church and state
   c.   Religious and social intolerance
   d.   Renaissance admiration for the Greeks and Romans

7.   Diderot's opinions on sexuality included

   a.   A defense of homosexuality
   b.   The importance of ritual and tradition in marriage
   c.   An advocacy of strict and complete monogamy
   d.   The renunciation of chastity for the unmarried

8.   Cesare Baccaria challenged his century's and society's attitude toward

   a.   Church-state relations
   b.   Crime and punishment
   c.   Free love
   d.   Popular election of governmental officials

9.   Identify the correct relationship between the social scientist and his work.

   a.   Cesare Beccaria—advocated capital punishment as the most effective deterrent to crime
   b.   Francois Quesnay—tried to discover the natural economic laws governing society
   c.   Adam Smith—advocated a state control of the economy for maximum profits
   d.   David Hume—tried to discover the natural laws of social sexuality

10.   In his *Social Contract*, Rousseau expressed the belief that

   a.   Government is an evil that should be eliminated
   b.   The will of the individual is all-important
   c.   We achieve freedom by following what is best for all
   d.   A child is a small adult with all the same abilities and obligations

11.   In the Eighteenth Century it was understood that in salons

   a.   No man would be admitted without a female companion
   b.   Sexual relations were more important than intellectual conversation
   c.   No women would ever be admitted
   d.   Relations between men and women would be purely platonic

12.   Rococo architecture of the Eighteenth Century was

    a.   Largely confined to France
    b.   Best expressed in the work of Baron d'Holbach
    c.   Best expressed in the work of Balthasar Neumann
    d.   Characterized by strict geometrical patterns

13.   European music of the Eighteenth Century was exemplified by

    a.   Amadeus Mozart, who shifted the musical focus from Italy to Austria
    b.   G.F.W. Handel, a prince who composed as a hobby
    c.   The elitist, aristocratic world of Haydn
    d.   The loosely woven, secular odes of Bach

14.   Which of the following trends is true of historical literature of the Eighteenth Century?

    a.   It exhibited a growing preoccupation with politics
    b.   It was more social science than literature
    c.   It paid close attention to the economic and social causes of historical events
    d.   It generally praised the Middle Ages

15.   During the Eighteenth Century the British were the acknowledged pioneers in

    a.   The Rococo style in architecture
    b.   The novel as a vehicle for fiction
    c.   The Baroque style in music
    d.   The prison reform that swept Europe a century later

16.   Most of the eighteenth-century European universities were

    a.   Centers of innovation and intellectual adventure
    b.   Completely secular institutions
    c.   Elitist and geared to the needs of the upper class
    d.   Concerned primarily with vocational education

17.   A noticeable trend in eighteenth-century medicine was

    a.   Dramatic improvement in hospital care
    b.   A decline in practices like bleeding
    c.   A lessening of the old distinction between surgeons and physicians
    d.   The eradication of traditional forms of faith healing

18.   Literacy rates in late eighteenth-century Europe

    a.   Were about equal for men and women
    b.   Were distributed evenly across class lines
    c.   Were generally higher than earlier
    d.   Were in decline from the previous century

19.   Because of its growing influence, the Society of Jesus was in 1773

    a.   Given a new charter in keeping with its success
    b.   Granted land in perpetuity in the Papal States
    c.   Cut down to half its size in order to increase efficiency
    d.   Dissolved by order of the pope

20.   Most eighteenth-century Christians believed that the solution to the "Jewish problem" was

    a.   Complete religious tolerance in each nation
    b.   Conversion to the Christian faith
    c.   Exile to the Americas or Africa
    d.   Camps for mass extermination

Complete the Following Sentences:

1.   Pierre Bayle paved the way for the philosophes by attacking in his book, _____
_____ _____ _____, superstition, intolerance, and
_____.

2.   Using the format of two Persians, supposedly visiting Europe, Montesquieu criticized the two
main French institutions, the _____ _____ and the
_____. In his *Spirit of the Laws* he praised British government for its
_____ and _____.

3.   Voltaire, whose religious faith is termed _____, fought for religious tolerance
and justice in the murder case of Protestant _____ _____.

4.   Diderot's great multivolume contribution to the Enlightenment, his _____, was
attacked by censors for establishing "a spirit of _____ and _____,"
but had widespread influence when in later editions its _____ was reduced.

5.   Among the Physiocrats, Scotsman Adam Smith criticized the economic _____ of his day, while Frenchman Francois Quesney said _____ was the greatest source of wealth.

6.   Jean-Jacque Rousseau's interests roamed from government in his book *The* _____ _____ to education in _____; and he blamed _____ _____ for the inequality of human society.

7.   Rococo's grace is illustrated by Watteau's lyrical portrayals of _____ life and Newmann's pilgrimage church of the _____.

8.   Music lovers today still celebrate the genius of Handel's great oratorio, *The* _____, and Mozart's "black comedy," _____ _____.

9.   The writing of history during the Enlightenment was given stature by Voltaire's study of the age of _____ and Gibbon's study of the decline and fall of the _____ _____.

10.   Although the Jesuits gained great influence by directing the _____ of young aristocrats, their image as an international network that threatened governments led to their expulsion from _____, _____, and _____.

Place the Following in Chronological Order and Give Dates:

1.   Publication of Adam Smith's *Wealth of Nations*   1.

2.   Publication of Rousseau's *Social Contract*   2.

3.   Publication of Montesquieu's *Persian Letters*   3.

4.   Publication of Condorcet's *Progress of the Human Mind*   4.

5.   Gibbon's *Decline and Fall of the Roman Empire* completed   5.

6.   Diderot's *Encyclopedia* begun   6.

7.   Publication of Voltaire's *Philosophic Letters*   7.

Questions for Critical Thought:

1.   Discuss the intellectual changes in Europe during the Seventeenth Century which culminated in the Enlightenment of the Eighteenth Century.

2.   Name the major Enlightenment philosophes, and summarize what each of them contributed to the movement.

3.   What was the "New Science of Man" that arose during the Enlightenment? What were its roots, and what did it add to man's self-awareness?

4.   Describe innovations in art, music, and literature during the Enlightenment. How did Enlightenment philosophy encourage and mold these innovations?

5.   What observations about women made by Mary Wollstoncraft in 1792 do you hear being stressed by feminists today, two centuries later?

6.   Through what media and in what forms did the ideas of the philosophes reach the better educated members of the general public?

7.   At the same time that the philosophes were working to change the world, what was going on among the masses? Describe "popular" culture at the time of the Enlightenment.

8.   What happened to the various "state churches" of Europe under the attacks of the Enlightenment critics?

9.   Describe popular religion—as opposed to institutional religions—during the Eighteenth Century. Why were the masses relatively unresponsive or hostile to the philosophes' attacks on religion?

Analysis of Primary Source Documents:

1.   Summarize Montesquieu's theory of the separation of government powers, and show how he affected the thinking of those who created the American republic to come.

2.   Explain how and why Voltaire's attack on Christian intolerance proved effective. How might an orthodox Christian defend against such attacks?

3.   Demonstrate with Diderot's *Voyage* the way the philosophes considered their thinking both highly sophisticated and "naturally" simple.

4.   Briefly state the two arguments: a) that Rousseau's "general will" leads to democracy; b) that it leads to totalitarianism. What do you think?

5.   Show how Mary Wollstonecraft appealed both to men and to women in her call for the rights of woman. What kinds of people (men and women) would have responded favorably and what kinds would have responded unfavorably to her arguments?

6.   From descriptions of Enlightenment salons and relations between philosophes and hostesses, what portrait of the intellectual woman of the Eighteenth Century emerges? Do you approve of this woman? Why or why not?

7.   What reasons does the historian Edward Gibbon give for his general optimism about the future of the human race? What evidence do you find in his writings that he considers Europe the center of civilization?

8.   Defend, as some eighteenth-century judge might, the punishment inflicted on criminals, as recorded by Restif de la Bertonne. Then critique it.

9.   Describe the church services conducted by John Wesley and his Methodists. Explain why Wesley's Church of England did not welcome this movement.

THE EIGHTEENTH CENTURY: EUROPEAN STATES, INTERNATIONAL WARS, AND SOCIAL CHANGE

Chapter Outline:

I.   The European States in the Eighteenth Century
    A.   Enlightened Absolutism?
        1.   The Concept of Natural Rights
        2.   A Call for Enlightened Rulers
    B.   The Atlantic Seaboard States
        1.   France and the Long Rule of Louis XV
        2.   Great Britain and the Relations of King to Parliament
            a.   The Rise of Prime Ministers
            b.   The Case of John Wilkes
        3.   The Decline of the Dutch Republic
    C.   Absolutism in Central and Eastern Europe
        1.   Prussia and Its Junkers
        2.   Austrian Empire and Its Enlightened Habsburgs
        3.   Russia Under Catherine the Great
        4.   The Destruction of Poland
    D.   The Mediterranean World
        1.   Occasional Sparks of Rebirth in Spain and Portugal
        2.   Austrian Domination of Italy
    E.   Scandinavia
    F.   Enlightened Absolutism Revisited
        1.   Its Rarity and Brevity
        2.   The Barriers of Reality

II.   Wars and Diplomacy in the Eighteenth Century
    A.   The War of the Austrian Succession (1740-1748)
        1.   The Vulnerability of Maria Theresa
        2.   The Weak Peace of Aix-la-Chapelle

B. The Seven Years' War (1756-1763)
    1. The European Theater
    2. The War for Empire
    3. The British Victory
C. Armies and Warfare
    1. Class Divisions of the Armies
    2. Dramatic Increases in Size of Armies

III. Economic Expansion and Social Change
    A. Growth of the European Population
        1. A Falling Death Rate
        2. Improvements in Diet
        3. Little Improvement in Hygiene
        4. Lingering Outbreaks of Disease
    B. Family, Marriage, and Birthrate Patterns
        1. The Nuclear Family as Normative
        2. A More "Enlightened" Treatment of Children Among the Rich
        3. The Continued Suffering of Poor Children
        4. Late Marriages
        5. Women, Children, and Family Income
    C. A Revolution in Agriculture?
        1. An Increase in Land Under Cultivation
        2. A Greater Supply of Meat
        3. Scientific Experiments and Agricultural Techniques
    D. New Methods of Finance and Industry
        1. National Banks
        2. "Bubbles" that Burst
        3. Textiles and Cottage Industries
        4. Richard Arkwright and Mechanized Production
    E. Toward a Global Economy: Mercantile Empires and Worldwide Trade
        1. Colonial Empires
            a. Portuguese and Spanish Decline
            b. British and French Growth
            c. The Far East
        2. Global Trade: Slavery and its Opponents

IV. The Social Order of the Eighteenth Century
    A. The Peasants
        1. Domination by Wealthy Landowners
        2. The Village As Center of Culture
        3. Poor Diet

B. The Nobility
    1. Military Service
    2. The Country House
    3. The Grand Tour
C. The Inhabitants of Towns and Cities
    1. Urban Oligarchies
    2. A Growing Middle Class
    3. Laborers
    4. Poverty and Its Opponents

Chapter Summary:

While Europe experienced the scientific and intellectual revolutions of the Seventeenth and Eighteenth Centuries, its various states moved from early modern absolutism to the verge of republican revolution. Across the continent the Old Regimes were experiencing their last set of crises in what can now be seen as preparation for the convulsions that would usher in the modern age.

It was a time of what has been called "enlightened absolutism," although how enlightened the rulers were depends on the nation being studied. In Britain and Holland kingship gave way to representative government, even if those being represented were the upper classes, while in France and Eastern Europe various forms of absolutism continued. In Prussia, for example, the Hohenzollerns gave their people efficiency and military glory without granting them civil rights, while in Austria the Emperor Joseph II tried to make liberal Philosophy his lawmaker—but in the end believed he had failed.

Warfare became much more efficient during the Eighteenth Century; and wars defined the future even more than they had in the century before. Prussia took its place as one of the strong nation-states because of its performance in the War of the Austrian Succession. Britain won the war for overseas empire with its victory over France in the Seven Years' War.

Meanwhile populations continued to grow, and improvements in agriculture production and the riches of overseas colonies increased national prosperity in most countries. Yet the gap between rich and poor grew ever more pronounced, and poverty virtually overwhelmed organizations and governments that tried to do something to remedy it. The stage was set for social revolution and the military strife that usually follows it.

Identify:

1. Enlightened Absolutism

2. Duke of Orleans

3. Fleury

4. United Kingdom

5. Pocket borough

6. Hanoverians

7. Robert Walpole

8. Patriots

9. General Directory

10. Joseph II

11. Emelyan Pugachev

12. Thaddeus Kosciuszko

13. Pragmatic Sanction

14. Robert Clive

15. Enclosure

16. Cottage industry

17. Richard Arkwright

18. Grand Tour

19. Uffizi Gallery

20. Order of St. Vincent de Paul

Match the Following Words with their Definitions:

1. Marie Antoinette

2. Robert Walpole

3. John Wilkes

4. Junkers

5. Maria Theresa

6. Jethro Tull

7. Richard Arkwright

8. Society of Friends

9. Andrea Palladio

10. Sisters of Charity

A. Austrian empress who led political and fiscal reforms

B. Agriculture experimenter who advocated keeping soil loose for air and moisture

C. Architect whose classical style influenced country homes of aristocrats

D. Austrian wife of French King Louis XVI

E. Religious group that excluded slave owners from membership

F. Catholic organization dedicated to helping the poor

G. Prussian ruling class who held most army offices

H. Inventor of the "water frame" powered spinning wheel

I. British prime minister George I and II permitted to run their governments

J. Journalist members of the British parliament whose quarrel with royalty led to reform

Choose the Correct Answer:

1. France in the Eighteenth Century

    a. Prospered under the enlightened philosophe Louis XV
    b. Suffered severe economic depression throughout the century
    c. Was torn apart by civil wars
    d. Lost an empire and acquired a huge public debt

2. Political developments in eighteenth-century Britain included

   a. Parliament taking over the last remaining powers of the monarchy
   b. The rearranging of boroughs to make elections to the Commons more fair
   c. Calls for reform after the corrupt prime ministership of Pitt the Younger
   d. The increasing influence and power of the king's ministers to make public policy

3. The British aristocracy of the Eighteenth Century

   a. Was split into two sharply divided groups in the House of Lords and House of Commons
   b. Allowed the monarchy to maintain some power because of its own factional struggles
   c. Lost many seats in Parliament to the growing merchant class of politicians
   d. Won seats on both houses through an equitable system of popular election

4. A continuing trend through the Eighteenth Century in Prussia was

   a. That the bureaucracy was out of control
   b. The social and military dominance of the Junkers
   c. A reluctance to get involved in European wars
   d. Social mobility for peasants through civil service

5. Frederick the Great of Prussia succeeded in

   a. Imposing his strict Protestantism on his populace
   b. Crushing the power of the Prussian nobility
   c. Carrying out all the philosophes' calls for reform
   d. Creating greater unity for Prussia's scattered lands

6. The War of the Austrian Succession was caused by the fact that in 1740 the heir to the Austrian throne was a

   a. Woman
   b. Child
   c. Catholic
   d. Protestant

7. Under Joseph II, the Austrian Empire

   a. Reversed the enlightened reforms of Maria Theresa
   b. Rescinded all of Hungary's privileges
   c. Saw the nobility's power taken away forever
   d. Saw popular discontent rise because of drastic reforms

8.   Joseph II's reforms included all of the following *except*

   a.   Complete religious toleration
   b.   The abolition of serfdom
   c.   The construction of internal trade barriers
   d.   Establishment of the principle of equality of all before the law

9.   Russia's Catherine the Great

   a.   Followed successfully a policy of expansion against the Turks
   b.   Instigated enlightened reforms for the peasantry after the Pugachev revolt
   c.   Alienated the nobility with her extensive enlightened reforms
   d.   Had two of her sons assassinated to prevent their further plotting against her

10.   The late eighteenth-century partition of Poland

   a.   Occurred after decades of warfare between its neighbors
   b.   Was overturned by Thaddeus Kosciuszko
   c.   Showed that a nation in those days needed a strong king
   d.   All of the above

11.   Enlightened absolutism in the Eighteenth Century

   a.   Never completely overcame the political and social realities of the day
   b.   Was most successful in strengthening administrative systems in the nation-states
   c.   Was limited to policies that did not undermine the interests of the nobility
   d.   All of the above

12.   The European theater of the Seven Years' War witnessed

   a.   A combined force of Austrian, Russian, and French troops defeated by Prussia
   b.   The victory of Frederick the Great at the Battle of Rossbach in Saxony
   c.   An end to the dream of an European balance of power
   d.   The recognition of Russian territorial gains under the peace of Huberstusburg

13.   European warfare in the Eighteenth Century was characterized by

   a.   A continued reliance on mercenary armies on the mainland
   b.   Ideological fervor that led to bloody battles
   c.   Limited objectives and elaborate maneuvers
   d.   Massive direct confrontations and pitched battles

14. The "agricultural revolution" of the Eighteenth Century

   a.   Depended on the emergence of the open field system
   b.   Occurred despite an absence of new crops
   c.   Was best suited to large farmers who could make use of new agricultural techniques
   d.   Was resisted by aristocrats like Jethro Tull

15. Which of the following statements best applies to Europe's social order in the Eighteenth Century?

   a.   It differed from the Middle Ages in that wealth was the sole determining factor in a person's social standing
   b.   The nobility was homogeneous and served the same social function throughout Europe
   c.   Peasants were still hindered by a variety of feudal services and fees imposed by powerful nobles
   d.   Peasants and nobles grew closer socially in eastern Europe, where serfdom was eradicated

16. European society of the Eighteenth Century witnessed

   a.   Earlier marriages
   b.   The continued dominance of the nuclear family
   c.   A decline in the importance of the woman in the family's economy
   d.   Laws that ended infanticide and illegitimacy

17. Europe's overseas slave trade in the Eighteenth Century

   a.   Declined from its seventeenth century high
   b.   Was perhaps the most profitable part of international trade
   c.   Was gradually phased out because it was unprofitable
   d.   Was used primarily to supply colonies with domestic slaves

18. The Eighteenth Century European nobility

   a.   Played a large role in administering nation-states
   b.   Lost its old dominance in military affairs
   c.   Composed twenty percent of Europe's population
   d.   Differed little in wealth and power from state to state

19. The English nobility's country houses

    a. Were secondary in importance to London town houses
    b. Architecturally reflected individualistic trends
    c. Reflected a growing male dominance
    d. Replaced the Grand Tour as a setting for the education of young male nobles

20. The problem of poverty in eighteenth-century Europe

    a. Was most chronic in Britain, which had no poor relief
    b. Was solved by private religious organizations
    c. Was made worse because government officials were generally hostile to the poor
    d. Was solved in France by public works projects

Complete the Following Sentences:

1. Because many seats in the British Parliament were controlled by one man—seats from what were called _____ boroughs—the House of Commons was dominated by the _____ aristocracy.

2. William Pitt the Younger served King _____ through the times of the _____ Revolution and wars of _____.

3. Frederick the Great of Prussia loved learning so much that he invited the writer _____ to live in his court; and he sought to be enlightened by granting his people freedom of _____ and _____ and religious _____.

4. When Joseph II of Austria succeeded his mother _____ _____ as sole ruler, he announced that _____ was the lawmaker of his empire.

5. The peasants' revolt against Catherine the Great of Russia was led by the Cossack _____ _____, who was finally _____, after which Catherine treated as treason any suggestion of _____ _____.

6. In 1772 Poland was partitioned and lost _____% of its land and _____% of its people. _____ more partitions followed within a quarter century.

7. Outside Europe the Seven Years' War was fought in _____ and _____ _____ to see whether Britain or France would have the greater _____.

8. Rousseau's theories about children may have helped influence upper class women to abandon the use of _____ to feed their babies and to begin buying _____ and _____ designed for children.

9. European nations sought colonies in the West Indies to provide them with tobacco, _____, _____, and _____, all raised by _____ labor.

10. The young English aristocrat on his Grand Tour is said to have stopped in Paris to learn how to act _____, in Florence to see _____, and in Venice to meet _____.

Place the Following in Chronological Order and Give Dates:

1. Joseph II joins Maria Theresa to rule Austria   1.

2. The Seven Years' War   2.

3. The Hanoverian Succession in Britain   3.

4. Regicide of Louis XVI   4.

5. First Partition of Poland   5.

6. Frederick the Great begins reign in Prussia   6.

7. William Pitt the Younger retires   7.

Questions for Critical Thought:

1. Define the term "Enlightened Despotism." Give three examples of enlightened despots of the Eighteenth Century, show why they were given the title, and indicate how enlightened each one was.

2. Describe the events and personalities that moved Britain during the Eighteenth Century from absolute to limited monarchy. Why did the same process not take place in France?

3. List three Central and Eastern European monarchies of the Eighteenth Century, and explain why or why not each of them is counted a success.

4.   Discuss war and diplomacy in the Eighteenth Century, and show how they differed from war and diplomacy in earlier European centuries.

5.   Describe the causes and results of the Seven Years' War. Explain why and how it was decisive for the colonial ambitions of Britain and France.

6.   Describe daily life in the Eighteenth Century, particularly marriage, the family, and the treatment of children.

7.   Discuss the progress made in eighteenth-century agriculture. What were the good and bad sides of such progress for peasants?

8.   Contrast the lives of nobles and peasants in the Eighteenth Century. What factors prevented major social upheavals until late in the period?

9.   Describe the peculiar phenomenon known as The Grand Tour. What purpose did it serve, and what did it generally accomplish?

10. How did thinking people of the Eighteenth Century explain the great poverty of their age, and what remedies did they suggest?

Analysis of Primary Source Documents:

1.   Describe Louis XVI's nightly *coucher*. What was the purpose of such a ritual? What was the method behind his madness?

2.   After reading the correspondence between Frederick of Prussia and his father, how would you think he probably described "the old man" to trusted friends his own age?

3.   Outline and explain the implications of Catherine the Great's proposals for a new Russian law code. In what sense do her guidelines place her in the category of "enlightened despot," and how does she fall short?

4.   How would you know, even without being told, that the battle account from Quebec in 1759 was written by an Englishman? How would a French soldier have told it differently?

5.   What clues do you find in Arthur Young's *Travels* that he may have arranged his "findings" to fit the argument for English agricultural practices he intended to make from the start?

6.   How does the British Woolen Workers' Petition of 1786 reflect the two conflicting definitions of "progress" in that day?

7.   What do contemporary descriptions of slave trading tell you about white attitudes toward blacks? To what degree did they and did they not consider slaves humans?

8.   Describe a debate that might have occurred between an advocate of free market economy and one who believes in government programs to help the poor in eighteenth-century France.

A REVOLUTION IN POLITICS: THE ERA OF THE FRENCH REVOLUTION AND NAPOLEON

Chapter Outline:

I. The Beginnings of the Revolutionary Age: The American Revolution
  A. The British Attempt to Reorganize the American Empire
    1. New Taxes
    2. Colonial Resistance: Arguments Over Representation
    3. Acts of Rebellion: The Boston Tea Party
  B. The War for American Independence
    1. Declaration of Independence
    2. European Aid After Saratoga
    3. Victory at Yorktown
  C. Toward a New Nation
    1. Its Constitution
    2. Its Bill of Rights
  D. The American Revolution's Impact on Europe
    1. Stories of the Success of Freedom
    2. Respect for the Bill of Rights

II. The French Revolution
  A. Its Background
    1. Class Grievances
      a. Privileges of the Clergy and Nobility
      b. A Rising Middle Class Without Power
    2. A Financial Emergency
    3. From Estates-General to a National Assembly
    4. The Common People Intervene
  B. The Destruction of the Old Regime
    1. Declaration of the Rights of Man and the Citizen
    2. The King and the Church
    3. A New Constitution
    4. Opposition from Abroad

C.   The Radical Revolution
     1.   Proclamation of a Republic
     2.   Execution of Louis XVI
     3.   A Nation in Arms
     4.   Committee of Public Safety and the Reign of Terror
     5.   "Republic of Virtue"
     6.   Dechristianization and A New Calendar
D.   Reaction and the Directory

III. The Age of Napoleon
A.   His Rise to Power
     1.   Military Victory in Italy and Losses in Egypt
     2.   Consulship (1799-1804)
     3.   Emperor (1804-1815)
B.   The Domestic Policies of Emperor Napoleon
     1.   Concordat with the Church
     2.   The Code Napoleon
     3.   Centralization of Administration
C.   Napoleon's Empire and Europe's Response
     1.   The Three Divisions: France, Dependent States, Allied States
     2.   Obedience and Liberties
     3.   Destruction of the Old Order
     4.   Europe's Reaction
          a.   British Resistance
          b.   Nationalism
          c.   The Russian Fiasco
          d.   Elba, Waterloo, and St. Helena

Chapter Summary:

The late Eighteenth Century saw the coming of revolutions long overdue, revolutions that would combine the ideals of the philosophes with the frustrations of social and economic groups long denied equal rights and powers in the nation-states. Europe and indeed the world would never be the same again.

The revolution began, of all places, in the British colonies along the American east coast. Pushed to rebellion by a growing dissatisfaction with the way Britain administered their affairs for them, the colonists declared their independence and to the world's surprise, but not without the world's help, made good on their boasts. They tried with some success to establish a republic based on the theories of the Enlightenment. The example was not lost on Europeans.

Within a decade of America's independence, when Louis XVI of France called his Estates-

General to help him raise revenues, the Third Estate declared itself a national Assembly and proceeded to initiate the French Revolution. Through the rest of the century France led the way to a reordering of the Old Regime and incurred the wrath of all the kings of Europe. When the radical phase of the revolution went too far and France found herself beset with enemies on every side, a conservative reaction set in and led to the rise of the liberal dictator who made himself emperor of the French, Napoleon Bonaparte.

For a decade Napoleon remade the map of Europe, using military genius to bring the liberal ideals of the revolution to the nations he conquered. Even after he was defeated and exiled, after royal figures were restored to their thrones, the spirit of the French Revolution lived on to inspire succeeding generations. The world in which we live was truly born in these revolutions of the late Eighteenth and early Nineteenth Centuries.

Identify:

1. Stamp Act

2. Tea Act

3. *Common Sense*

4. Saratoga

5. Confederation Congress

6. Nobility of the Robe

7. Nobility of the Sword

8. Ségur Law

9. Estates-General

10. National Assembly

11. Declaration of the Rights of Man

12. Paris Commune

13. Maximilien Robespierre

14. Committee of Public Safety

15. Temple of Reason

16. Reign of Terror

17. Thermidorean Reaction

18. *Code Napoleon*

19. Elba

20. St. Helena

Match the Following Words with their Definitions:

1. Coercive Acts

2. Articles of Confederation

3. Lafayette

4. Bastille

5. Jacobins

6. Sans-culottes

7. Temple of Reason

8. Thermidor

9. Concordat

10. Trafalgar

A. General who fought with the Americans to "strike a blow against England"

B. Party of radical deputies in the National Assembly

C. The revolutionary name for Notre Dame Cathedral

D. Closed the Port of Boston until colonists paid for destroyed tea

E. Naval battle which led Napoleon to adopt the Continental System

F. The month in which the French Revolution took a conservative turn

G. Paris prison which became the symbol of royal oppression

H. Leaders of the Paris Commune, mostly tradesmen and artisans

I. Napoleon's agreement with the Catholic Church

J. The first American constitution

Choose the Correct Answer:

1. After 1763 British authorities and American colonists came into conflict over

    a. Expansion west of the Appalachians
    b. Expansion south of the Rio Grande
    c. Freedom of religious expression
    d. Treatment of French prisoners of war

2. The British Tea Act was devised to

    a. Stimulate the American economy
    b. Provoke the Americans to war
    c. Bail out the British East India Company
    d. Standardize the quality of tea

3. The American War for Independence from Britain

    a. Was won despite British victories in most battles
    b. Was won with superior battlefield forces
    c. Was won by better trained officers
    d. Was won with minimal European support

4. The French entered the war for American independence after

    a. A visit to Paris by George Washington
    b. A British victory at Yorktown
    c. A personal plea by Thomas Jefferson
    d. An American victory at Saratoga

5. The British were forced to surrender to the Americans largely because of

    a. Lack of support from the people of England
    b. The intervention of European nations and fear of a wider war with them
    c. The military superiority of the Americans
    d. An outbreak of the Bubonic Plague in London which reduced the number of military
        volunteers

6. The United States Constitution of 1789

    a. Was a revision of the Articles of Confederation
    b. Was viewed by European liberals as too utopian to last
    c. Depended heavily on the political theories of Montesquieu
    d. Had little or no influence on the French Revolution

7. By the Eighteenth Century the French nobility and bourgeoisie were

    a. Growing farther apart in social status
    b. Increasingly less distinguishable from each other
    c. Rapidly losing social status to the peasants
    d. Frequently involved in street fights

8. The immediate cause of the French Revolution was

    a. Military losses against Britain
    b. A series of financial reversals
    c. Religious turmoil
    d. The ideas of the philosophes

9. The controversy over voting by order rather than voting by head in the Estates-General
    meeting led to

    a. A motion by the Nobles of the Robe to adjourn
    b. A move by "lovers of liberty" to block voting by head
    c. The expulsion of the Third Estate
    d. The withdrawal of the Third Estate to form a National Assembly

10. The Declaration of the Rights of Man and Citizen

    a. Was written by Louis XVI to extend civil rights
    b. Was rejected by philosophes
    c. Owed much to the American Declaration of Independence
    d. Kept all aristocratic privileges intact

11. The Jacobins were named for

    a. The revolutionary leader Jacques Boulanger
    b. The brother of Louis XVI
    c. The Old Testament patriarch who led his Hebrew people out of Egyptian slavery
    d. The Paris convent where they first met

12. In the Reign of Terror's "preservation" of the revolution from its internal enemies

    a.   The nobility was singled out for total annihilation
    b.   Rebellious cities were brutally crushed by the army
    c.   No more than a total of 5,000 were killed at the guillotine
    d.   The Committee of Public Safety played little part

13. The new republican calendar of 1793

    a.   Named days and months after former kings
    b.   Was part of an effort at dechristianization
    c.   Was well received by most of the people
    d.   Was kept until Napoleon's defeat in 1815

14. The role of French women in the revolution

    a.   Was minimal and insignificant
    b.   Was on the whole encouraged by men
    c.   Was limited only to bread riots
    d.   Was kept outside the political sphere

15. The program of dechristianization did *not* include

    a.   A new secular calendar
    b.   Removal of saints' names from street signs
    c.   A systematic execution of bishops
    d.   Changing the names of church buildings

16. During the Thermidorean Reaction, the Directory

    a.   Relied primarily on the support of royalists
    b.   Was elected directly by universal franchise
    c.   Had wise and honest economic leadership
    d.   Relied primarily on the military for its survival

17. Which of the following statements best applies to Napoleon?

    a.   He was a child both of the Enlightenment and the Revolution
    b.   He had a deep sense of moral responsibility to the people of France
    c.   He advocated an invasion of Britain in the 1770s
    d.   He was born the son of a Parisian priest

18. Which of the following statements best applies to Napoleon's domestic policies?

    a.   Great autonomy was given to provincial administrations
    b.   His "new aristocracy" was still based on wealth and privilege as well as birth
    c.   His Civil Code reaffirmed the ideals of the Revolution while creating a uniform legal system
    d.   He reestablished Catholicism as the official state religion

19. Napoleon's Grand Empire

    a.   Was composed of three parts but united under him
    b.   Revived the power of the nobility and clergy everywhere
    c.   Included all of Europe after 1805
    d.   Had no long-lasting impact on the conquered countries

20. Napoleon's Continental System tried to defeat Britain by

    a.   A massive invasion across the English Channel
    b.   Preventing Britain from trading freely
    c.   Fomenting civil war in Scotland
    d.   Giving arms to the Irish Republican Army

Complete the Following Sentences:

1. Britain's first scheme to raise money for defense of its American lands, the _____ of 1765, was quickly repealed. Reaction to an Act in 1773 concerning a tax on _____ turned violent.

2. Spurred on by the arguments of _____ _____ in *Common Sense*, the _____ Continental Congress declared independence from Britain on July 4, _____.

3. Hoping the Estates-General would help him raise _____, Louis XVI called it into session at _____ in May, 1789, opening the way for the French _____.

4. Under the Civil Constitution of the Clergy, bishops and priests were to be elected by the _____ and paid by the _____ and had to take an oath of allegiance to the _____ _____.

5. In debates over the fate of Louis XVI, the _____ faction favored keeping him alive while the _____ called for his execution, and the _____ won.

6. The movement of dechristianization removed the prefix _____ from street signs, changed the name of the Cathedral of _____ _____, and urged priests to _____.

7. In the revolutionary calendar, months were named for natural, agricultural events, such as _____ for the misty time, _____ for planting seed, and _____ for ripening.

8. Robespierre's radical attempt to create the Republic of _____ led to his condemnation to death at the _____.

9. Napoleon attempted to strike indirectly at Britain in _____, which would block her route to India, but when he failed he _____ his army and returned to _____.

10. After his first exile on _____, Napoleon returned to rule France until his defeat at _____ and final exile on _____.

Place the Following in Chronological Order and Give Dates:

1. American Bill of Rights   1.

2. Battle of Waterloo   2.

3. Continental System Established   3.

4. Storming of the Bastille   4.

5. Declaration of American Independence   5.

6. Boston Tea Party   6.

7. Execution of Louis XVI   7.

Questions for Critical Thought:

1. Describe the sequence of events that led to the American Declaration of Independence from Britain. Explain why you think the episode was or was not inevitable.

2. Outline the system of government adopted by the American republic, and show why many Europeans considered it the fulfillment of Enlightenment dreams.

3. Describe French society and government just before the French Revolution. What characteristics were most responsible for the upheaval that began in 1789?

4. Outline the major events of the French Revolution from 1789 through 1804, and discuss four general principles of revolution to be found in this picture.

5. Why did the French Revolution turn radical? What forms did the radical phase take, and what were the final results?

6. What steps did the French revolutionaries take in 1783 through 1794 to ensure that there could be no return to the Old Regime? To what extent were they and were they not successful?

7. List and discuss the major events that brought Napoleon Bonaparte to power in France. At what points might he have been stopped? How?

8. Evaluate Napoleon as a military man and as a head of state. Did he fulfill or betray the revolution? Explain your conclusion.

9. Why did Napoleon fall? With your hindsight, how would you have advised him to avoid his demise? How successful do you feel you would have been advising him?

Analysis of Primary Source Documents:

1. Pretend you are a moderate member of the British Parliament and have just read the American Declaration of Independence. What would you say in your next speech to that body?

2. Describe the storming of the Bastille, and explain why this bloody event came to symbolize the French "triumph of justice and liberty."

3. What parts of the "Declaration of the Rights of Man" were derived from the writings of the philosophes, and what parts went beyond them?

4. What specific claims made by the "Declaration of the Rights of Woman" prevent one from mistakenly assuming that it is a document from the 1990s rather than the 1790s?

5. Use Anne Guinee's experience with the justice system during the reign of terror to show the insecurity of the regime that sought to make France a democracy.

6. It has been said that the words of Robespierre defending violence in the name of liberty could be the words of Lenin defending it in the name of communism. Explain how this might be true.

7. Pick out the words (nouns, adjectives, verbs) Napoleon used to create images and emotions that would inspire courage and determination among his men.

8. Which side would Napoleon have taken in the debate among historians: Does the age make the man or the man the age? How would he have defended his position?

Map Exercise 11: Napoleon's Empire

Using various shades of pencil, color and label the following:

1.   Austrian Empire
2.   Baltic Sea
3.   Bavaria
4.   Britain
5.   Confederation of the Rhine
6.   Corsica
7.   Denmark
8.   Elba
9.   France
10. Grand Duchy of Warsaw
11. Kingdom of Naples
12. Kingdom of Sicily
13. Prussia
14. Spain
15. Sweden
16. Switzerland

Pinpoint and label the following:

1.   Auerstadt
2.   Austerlitz
3.   Berlin
4.   Borodino
5.   Brussels
6.   Copenhagen
7.   Danzig
8.   Jena
9.   Kiev
10. Madrid
11. Marseilles
12. Milan
13. Moscow
14. Paris
15. Trafalgar
16. Ulm
17. Vienna
18. Waterloo

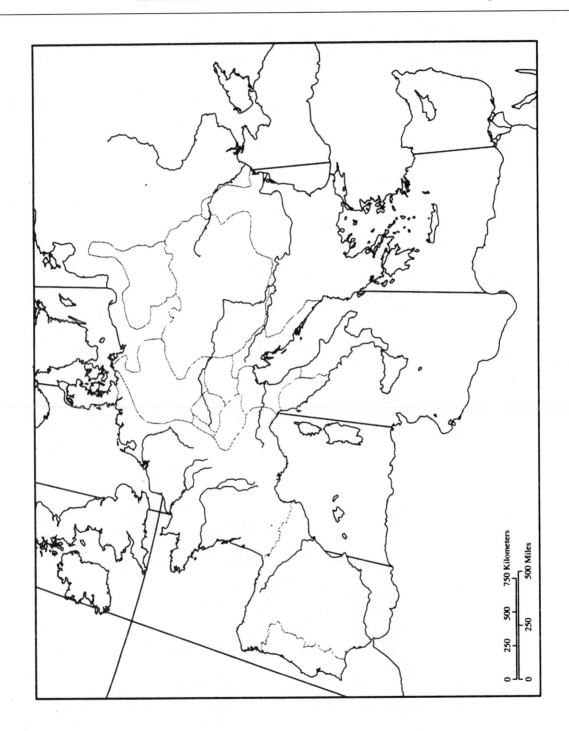

20 THE INDUSTRIAL REVOLUTION AND ITS IMPACT ON EUROPEAN SOCIETY

Chapter Outline:

I.   The Industrial Revolution in Great Britain
    A.   Its Origins and Causes
        1.   Capital for Investment
        2.   Mineral Resources
        3.   A Government Favorable to Business
        4.   Ready Markets
    B.   Technological Changes and New Forms of Industrial Organization
        1.   The Cotton Industry's Power Looms
        2.   James Watt's Steam Engine
        3.   The Iron Industry
        4.   Railroads: A Revolution in Transportation
            a.   Richard Trevithick's Locomotive
            b.   George Stephenson's *Rocket*
        5.   The Industrial Factory
    C.   The Great Exhibition of 1851
        1.   The Leadership of Prince Albert
        2.   Britain as Industrial Leader

II.   The Spread of Industrialism Beyond Britain
    A.   What Limited Its Spread
        1.   A Lack of Transportation Systems
        2.   Traditional Habits of Business
        3.   The Upheaval of Wars
        4.   Lack of Technical Education
    B.   What Encouraged Its Spread
        1.   Entrepreneurs with Technical and Business Skills
        2.   Technical Schools
        3.   Government Support
        4.   Joint-Stock Investment Banks

C. Centers of Continental Industrialization
   1. Belgium
   2. France
   3. Germany
D. The Industrial Revolution in the United States
   1. Building of a System of Transportation
   2. A Labor Supply from Rural New England
   3. The Capital-Intensive Pattern

III. The Social Impact of the Industrial Revolution
   A. Growth in Population
   B. Growth of Cities
      1. Irresponsible and Irresponsive Governments
      2. Wretched Sanitary Conditions
      3. Adulteration of Food
      4. The Reforms of Edwin Chadwick
   C. The New Industrial Middle Class
      1. Out of Mercantile Trades
      2. Out of Dissenting Religious Minorities
      3. To a New Elite
   D. The New Working Class
      1. As Laborers
      2. As Servants
      3. Their Working Conditions
         a. In the Mines
         b. Pauper Apprentices
         c. Child Labor
         d. Women Workers
         e. Factory Acts At Last
   E. Standards of Living for Workers
      1. Wild Fluctuations of Wages and Prices
      2. Periodic Overproduction and Unemployment
   F. Worker Efforts at Change
      1. Robert Owen's Utopian Socialism
      2. Trade Unions
      3. Luddite Attacks on Machinery
      4. Chartism's Petition to Parliament
   G. Government Efforts at Change
      1. Factory Act of 1833
      2. Coal Mines Act of 1842

Chapter Summary:

The Industrial Revolution that came first to Britain and then to the Continent of Europe changed the political and social order of Western people fully as much as the religious revolution called the Reformation, the intellectual revolution of the Enlightenment, or the political revolutions that followed the French Revolution. In many ways it changed the lives of the common worker more than any of the previous revolutions.

The Industrial Revolution started in Britain, where inventions, organizational skills, and natural resources combined to remake the countryside and the cities. It spread after a generation to the continent, particularly to places that had the same natural resources and organizational systems as Britain, and by the middle of the Nineteenth Century was redefining society throughout the Western world. The Great Exhibition of 1851 in London demonstrated the achievements but did not point out the human suffering that accompanied those achievements.

The social impact of the Industrial Revolution is still being observed and assessed. A tremendous growth in city populations, the creation of a new middle class and a working class, an ever increasing gap in earnings and quality of life between owners and workers all helped to make the modern age what it has been for a century—for better and for worse. The most striking losers in this new age were for many decades the children who were literally "used up" to supply labor for factories.

Eventually reaction came. The workers themselves, however limited their powers might be, began calling for more rights to determine their work and lives; and social reformers made the case of the workers so articulately that at last governments had to respond. The class struggle of modern times was underway.

Identify:

1. Capital

2. Daniel Defoe

3. Samuel Crompton

4. Thomas Newcomen

5. Henry Cort

6. Richard Trevithick

7. Rocket

8.   Great Exhibition

9.   Victoria and Albert

10. John Cockerill

11. Fritz Harkort

12. *Société Générale*

13. Rhineland

14. Harpers Ferry

15. Edwin Chadwick

16. Joshua Fielden

17. Robert Owen

18. Luddites

19. Chartism

20. Factory Acts

Match the Following Words with their Definitions:

1.	Edmund Cartwright	A.	Site of the Great Exhibition of 1851
2.	James Watt	B.	Site of Germany's rich coal resources
3.	George Stephenson	C.	Lawyer who championed the cause of the urban poor
4.	Crystal Palace	D.	Inventor of the power weaving loom
5.	Friedrich List	E.	Inventor of the steam engine
6.	*Crédit Mobilier*	F.	Advocate of rapid industrialization and the use of tariffs
7.	*Kreditanstalt*	G.	Industrial joint stock corporation of Vienna
8.	Ruhr Valley	H.	His *Rocket* was the first locomotive used on a public railway line
9.	Edwin Chadwick	I.	Industrial joint stock corporation of Paris
10.	Robert Owen	J.	Cotton magnate and social reformer whose ideas contributed to the trade union movement

Choose the Correct Answer:

1. The Industrial Revolution in Britain was in large part inspired by

    a. The urgent need to solve great urban poverty
    b. The failure of the cottage industry system
    c. Entrepreneurs who sought and accepted new manufacturing methods and inventions
    d. The great industrial success of the century before in Holland and France

2. The British industrial entrepreneur Richard Arkwright

    a. Typified the highly educated and mannered leader of the Industrial Revolution
    b. Invented the water frame spinning machine
    c. Perfected the Crompton's Mule
    d. Became Prime Minister

3. The steam engine was invented by

    a. James Watt of Scotland
    b. Richard Arkwright of Wales
    c. Edmund Cartwright of Ireland
    d. James Heriot of Yorkshire

4. The work ethic needed for efficient industrial production was taught as a religious virtue most noticeably in

    a. Catholic monasteries of northern England
    b. Lutheran gymnasia of western Germany
    c. Jewish synagogues of Poland
    d. Methodist meeting houses of the English midlands

5. In the Eighteenth Century Britain's cotton industry

    a. Could not keep pace with French textile production
    b. Was responsible for creating the first modern factories
    c. Declined due to the lack of technical innovations
    d. Went bankrupt due to gains in synthetic fiber production

6. The importance of railroads to the Industrial Revolution lay in the way they

    a. Increased British supremacy in civil and mechanical engineering
    b. Increased the size of markets and the price of goods in those markets
    c. Brought an end to joint-stock companies
    d. Ended the need for domestically produced coal

7. The new set of values established by factory owners during the Industrial Revolution

    a. Was rejected by evangelical religions as "unChristian"
    b. Was basically a continuation of the cottage system
    c. Was successfully challenged and never adopted by the working class
    d. Was destined to relegate the worker to a life of severe discipline

8. The Great Exhibition of 1851

   a. Showed how the Industrial Revolution had achieved human domination over nature
   b. Displayed Britain's industrial wealth and might to the world
   c. Was housed in the Crystal Palace, itself a tribute to British engineering skills
   d. All of the above

9. Continental industrialization differed from Britain's in that the continent

   a. Industrialized through the private capital of rich individuals like John Cockerill
   b. Was dependent upon joint-stock investment banks like the Crédit Mobilier
   c. Invested in the latest equipment and most productive mills
   d. Never established technical schools to train engineers and mechanics

10. The Industrial Revolution in the United States

    a. Never matched Britain's due to the lack of a system of internal transportation
    b. Employed large numbers of women in factories, especially in textile mills
    c. Utilized a labor-intensive system with many skilled workers
    d. Was limited mainly to the southern states

11. The "American System" benefitted the U.S. Industrial Revolution in that it

    a. Utilized America's large pool of artisans
    b. Forbade women and children from working in factories
    c. Revolutionized industrial production by saving labor
    d. Bridged the gap between the rich and the poor

12. American factory owners invested heavily in machinery because their work force was largely

    a. Female
    b. Young
    c. Skilled
    d. Unskilled

13. In 1842 Edwin Chadwick published a landmark study of British

    a. Poverty and urged greater sanitation
    b. Industrial profits and urged more mercantilism
    c. Schools and urged more instruction in ethics
    d. Fires and urged asbestos housing

14. The European population explosion of the Nineteenth Century

    a. Can be explained by increased birthrates
    b. Was largely caused by the disappearance of famine
    c. Was due to the absence of emigration
    d. Occurred despite the return of major epidemic diseases

15. The most dangerous working conditions in all of early industry were found in

    a. Meat packing plants
    b. Cotton mills
    c. Coal mines
    d. Shoe factories

16. Which of the following statements best applies to urban life in the early Nineteenth Century in Europe?

    a. Government intervention prevented consumer fraud and food contamination
    b. The decline in death rates accounted for increased populations in most large cities
    c. Lower-class family dwellings were on the whole much nicer than those in the countryside
    d. Filthy sanitary conditions were exacerbated by the refusal of city authorities to take responsibility

17. The largest group of European urban workers in the first half of the Nineteenth Century were

    a. Artisans and craftsmen
    b. Domestic servants
    c. Industrial workers
    d. Members of the guild

18. The harsh treatment of children in the workplace during the early Industrial Revolution

    a. Toughened and strengthened them physically for their adult lives
    b. Was in line with the brutal treatment of children in general
    c. Did not occur in mining operations, where children were never used because they were too small
    d. Was often prevented by parish officials who employed children as pauper apprentices only for clerical work

19. Before 1870 women's wages in textile mills were

    a.   The same as men's
    b.   Paid to their husbands
    c.   Half that of men's
    d.   Paid in foodstuffs

20. The Luddites

    a.   Received little local support from the people in their areas of activities
    b.   Physically attacked machines they believed adversely affected their livelihood
    c.   Were the lowest of unskilled workers in Britain
    d.   Were the first movement of the working classes on the continent

Complete the Following Sentences:

1. Britain led the Industrial Revolution because it had deposits of _____ and _____, because it had abundant _____, and because of its small _____.

2. The cotton industry was pushed forward dramatically by the water frame spinning machine of Richard _____ and the power loom of Edmund _____.

3. Richard Trevithick pioneered the use of the steam-powered _____, but Geroge Stephenson's _____ was the first used on a public line.

4. The Great Exhibition of 1851, held in the _____ _____ in _____, demonstrated that _____ led the world in industry.

5. Germany eventually played a major role in the industrial revolution because of _____ deposits in the _____ Valley of the _____.

6. In Ireland, where _____ peasants rented from absentee British _____ landlords, a mid-century _____ crop failure led to massive starvation.

7. As secretary for the _____ _____ Commission, Edwin Chadwick blamed urban diseases on _____ impurities and called for reforms in _____.

8.   Children were extensively used in factories because of their small _____ because they were easily _____ to work, and because they were a _____ supply of labor.

9.   The People's Charter of 1838 demanded universal suffrage for _____, that Members of Parliament be _____, and that Parliament meet _____.

10. The Factory Acts passed between 1802 and 1819 limited child labor to _____ hours a day, forbade hiring of children under _____, and required that children be taught _____ and _____ during work hours.

Place the Following in Chronological Order and Give Dates:

1.   Victoria and Albert's Great Exhibition   1.

2.   People's Charter promulgated   2.

3.   Cartwright invents the power loom   3.

4.   Watt invents the rotary steam engine   4.

5.   Ten Hours Act   5.

6.   Trevithick first uses the steam locomotive   6.

7.   Combination Acts repealed   7.

Questions for Critical Thought:

1.   What prior conditions brought about the First Industrial Revolution, and why did it come first to Great Britain?

2.   List the areas in which the Industrial Revolution enjoyed its most impressive successes. How did each field contribute to the overall pattern of technological progress?

3.   Explain how and why the Great Exhibition of 1851 came to symbolize the Industrial Revolution and Britain's place in it.

4. Show how and why the Continental Industrial Revolution differed from that of Britain. Why did it eventually surpass the productivity of its island competitor?

5. Show how and why the Industrial Revolution in the United States differed from both the British and the Continental ones. What factors favored eventual American superiority?

6. Discuss the social impact (the effect on daily life) of the Industrial Revolution. Show how we are still today living with its social consequences.

7. Describe the lifestyle of the new industrial middle class. Compare it to that of the industrial workers. What were the results of the widening economic gap of the Nineteenth Century?

8. Discuss the various reactions to industrial abuses. What remedies were offered, by whom were they offered, and how successful were they?

Analysis of Primary Source Documents:

1. List the traits Edward Baines said made Richard Arkwright a successful entrepreneur. Then list conditions, advantages, and probable personal traits that Baines failed to mention but which hindsight tells us also helped.

2. Describe the likely appearance and personality of a man or woman who had worked for five years under the rules of the Berlin Trading Company.

3. What commentary, hidden in his description of a steamship's arrival, was Mark Twain making about effects on American life of the Industrial Revolution? Is he for it or against it?

4. Pretend you are one of the few British members of Parliament sympathetic to the Irish and have just made a tour of their famine-stricken island. What would you tell Parliament to do?

5. What would you, a reform minded member of the British Parliament, have recommended the government do about child labor abuse? What would you have recommended as punishment for sadistic overseers?

6. Given the provocation they so often had, why do you suppose there were so few incidences of open rebellion among young industrial workers?

7. Although considered failures because they achieved no immediate results, what can you say of the Chartists' long-term and ultimate record?

REACTION, REVOLUTION, AND ROMANTICISM (1815-1850)

CHAPTER

21

Chapter Outline:

I. The Conservative Order, 1815-1830
    A. Peace Settlement After Napoleon
        1. Restoration of Kingdoms
        2. Containment of France
    B. The Conservative Ideology
        1. Edmund Burke's *Reflections* as Guide
        2. Joseph de Maistre's Concept of Order over Chaos
    C. The Conservative Dominion: The Concert of Europe
        1. From Quadruple to Quintuple Alliance
        2. Intervention by the Great Powers
        3. Revolt in Latin America
        4. The Greek Revolt, 1821-1832
    D. The Conservative Dominion: The European States
        1. Rule of the Tories in Britain
            a. The Peterloo Massacre
            b. Minor Reforms
        2. The Bourbon Restoration in France
            a. Louis XVIII's Moderation
            b. Charles X and the Revolt of 1830
        3. Intervention by the Powers in Italy and Spain
        4. Repression of Liberalism in Central Europe
            a. The *Burschenschaften* Movement Thwarted in Germany
            b. The Stagnation of Austria
        5. Tsarist Autocracy in Russia
            a. Speransky's Reforms
            b. The Decembrist Revolt
            c. The Reaction of Nicholas I

II. The Ideologies of Change
    A. Liberalism
        1. Limitations on Government
            a. Thomas Malthus on Population
            b. David Ricardo on Wages
        2. Civil Liberties for the Individual
        3. Legislative Power Over Monarchy
        4. Women's Rights
    B. Nationalism
    C. Early Socialism
        1. The Cooperative Community of Saint-Simon
        2. The Phalansteries of Charles Fourier
        3. Robert Owen's New Lanark
        4. Louis Blanc and State Socialism
        5. Flora Tristan's Synthesis of Socialism and Feminism

III. Revolution and Reform, 1830-1850
    A. Another French Revolution (1830)
        1. The Middle-Class Rule of Louis-Philippe
        2. Parties of Movement and Resistance
    B. Outbursts in Belgium, Poland, and Italy
    C. Reform in Britain
        1. The Whig Reform Act of 1832
        2. Repeal of the Corn Laws, in 1846
    D. Growth of the United States
        1. Jeffersonian Republicanism
        2. John Marshall and National Unity
        3. The Mass Democracy of Jackson
        4. The Abolitionist Movement
    E. The Revolutions of 1848
        1. Yet Another French Revolution: a Second Republic, a Second Bonaparte
        2. The Frankfurt Assembly in Germany
        3. Mazzini's *Risorgimento* in Italy
        4. The Failures of 1848

IV. The Emergence of An Ordered Society
    A. New Police Forces
        1. Louis-Maurice Debelleyme and Parisian *Serjents*
        2. Robert Peel and London "Bobbies"
        3. Berlin's *Schutzmannschaft*

   B.   Prison Reform
  1. A Decline in Exile
  2. Solitary Confinement

V. Culture in An Age of Reaction and Revolution: The Mood of Romanticism
   A.   Characteristics of Romanticism
  1. Sentiment and the Inner World: The Example of Goethe
  2. Individualism
  3. The Lure of the Middle Ages
  4. An Attraction to the Bizarre
   B.   Romantic Poets and the Love of Nature
  1. Percy Bysshe Shelley
  2. Lord Byron
  3. William Wordsworth
   C.   Romanticism in Art and Music
  1. Casper David Friedrich
  2. William Turner
  3. Eugene Delacroix
  4. Ludwig van Beethoven
  5. Hector Berlioz
   D.   The Revival of Religion
  1. Chateaubriand: Catholicism and the Harmony of All Things
  2. Protestant Evangelicalism and Personal Salvation

Chapter Summary:

The Congress of Vienna, which made peace at the end of the Napoleonic Wars, tried to restore the Old Order and its "legitimate" rulers. It tried to establish a conservative system, with a balance of power, that would give Europe peace as far as it could see into the future. It succeeded—for a time.

The conservative system was installed, but beneath a tranquil surface the barely suppressed ideals of liberty continued to stir up both hope and trouble. When combined with a rising call for independence and unification in nations long dependent and divided, it became a powerful agent of revolt and reform. Greece and the countries of Latin America threw off foreign masters. Revolts simmered and erupted finally in Russia, France, Austria, Germany, Belgium, Poland, and Italy. Some of them were successful, some were not; but together they made the first half of the Nineteenth Century a volatile time.

Intellectuals responded to the spirit of the times with various theories about human society. Men like Edmund Burke defended conservatism as the best system to preserve the institution that give people order and security, while Louis Blanc proposed a government-sponsored socialism to control the economy for the benefit of citizens. Some welcomed the continent-wide revolts of 1848, while some feared that political disintegration would soon follow, and perhaps both were surprised when the revolts led to more conservative regimes almost everywhere.

Yet reform did come, if not economic reform, certainly social. Police forces were created in major cities to keep order, and there were positive examples of prison reform. The reform movement had its cultural side, Romanticism, which brought forth a new generation of writers, artists, and musicians, all of them dedicated to a freedom unknown to the Classical Age of culture now passing away.

Identify:

1. Talleyrand

2. Metternich

3. Simón Bolivar

4. Tories

5. Peterloo

6. Michael Speransky

7. Decembrist Revolt

8. Charles Fourier

9. Louis Blanc

10. Flora Tristan

11. Louis-Philippe

12. William Lloyd Garrison

13. Giuseppe Mazzini

14. Bobbies

15. Romanticism

16. Goethe

17. Alexandre Dumas

18. J.M.W. Turner

19. Eugene Delacroix

20. Beethoven

Match the Following Words with their Definitions:

1.	Bourbons	A.	Party that attracted moneyed industrial groups
2.	Edmund Burke	B.	Advocated cooperative communities to solve economic problems
3.	Whigs	C.	Resulted in the overthrow of Louis-Philippe
4.	Thomas Malthus	D.	Their restoration fulfilled Metternich's principle of legitimacy
5.	David Ricardo		
6.	Saint-Simon	E.	Romantic artists with passion for color and exotic themes
7.	July Revolution	F.	Argued that wages rise only as population declines
8.	"June Days"		
9.	Robert Peel	G.	Sponsored bill to create London's Metropolitan Police Force
10.	Eugene Delacroix	H.	Spokesman for evolutionary conservatism
		I.	Resulted in the overthrow of Charles X
		J.	Argued that population growth mitigated against human progress

Choose the Correct Answer:

1. The Congress of Vienna

   a. Gave Prussia complete control over Polish lands
   b. Sought to maintain a balance of power among members of the Quadruple Alliance
   c. Failed to achieve a long-lasting peace among the nations of Europe
   d. Treated France leniently, particularly after Napoleon's One Hundred Days

2. Metternich

   a. Supported the revolutionary ideology of the French philosophes
   b. Believed that a free press was necessary to maintain personal liberties
   c. Held that all European monarchs shared a common interest in stability
   d. Was an atheist who supported the suppression of religion

3. The Quadruple Alliance became the Quintuple Alliance in 1818 with the addition of

   a. France
   b. Austria
   c. Britain
   d. Russia

4. Conservatism, which was the dominant political philosophy of Europe following the fall of Napoleon, was

   a. Rejected at Vienna by Metternich because it was inappropriate for the post-Napoleonic age
   b. Careful to protect the rights of the individual
   c. Best expressed intellectually by Edmund Burke in his *Reflections on the Revolution in France*
   d. Too radical for the liberal Joseph de Maistre, an evolutionary socialist

5. Under the Concert of Europe, Prince Metternich considered himself

   a. Fire chief in a dry season
   b. Chief priest of a new nationalist religion
   c. Honorary emperor of an international empire
   d. Minister of police in a dangerous world

6. The Concert of Europe was most successful at

    a. Ending the political domination of Greece by the Holy Alliance
    b. Thwarting Britain's attempts to intervene and crush revolts in Italy and Spain
    c. Crushing the colonial revolts in Latin America
    d. None of the above

7. The *Burschenschaften* or student societies of Germany wanted

    a. To spread German nationalism and comradeship
    b. To dismantle the armed forces of Germany
    c. A multi-ethnic European super state
    d. Regional concerns to dominate the political thinking of Germans

8. The growing forces of liberalism and nationalism in central Europe were best characterized by

    a. The reforms of Frederick William III of Prussia
    b. The affinity and unity of ethnic groups under Frederick II of Austria
    c. The liberal constitutions of the German Confederation states after 1815
    d. The *Burschenschaften*, the radical German student societies

9. David Ricardo wrote that in order to overcome the "iron law of wages" governments could

    a. Build cooperative farms for urban workers
    b. Do absolutely nothing because this was a law of nature
    c. Create a bureau of employment to control jobs
    d. Send their unemployable men to America

10. Identify the correct relationship between the economic liberal and his main idea.

    a. Samuel Smiles—"God helps those who help themselves"
    b. Adam Smith—"Misery and poverty are the result of the law of nature"
    c. David Ricardo—"Laissez-faire"
    d. Thomas Malthus—"iron law of wages"

11. The "Peterloo" demonstration and massacre were brought about by the high price of

    a. Beef in Prussia
    b. Ale in Austria
    c. Bread in Britain
    d. Textiles in France

12. Political reforms in Britain in the 1830s and 1840s included

   a. Relief to the unemployed through the Poor Law of 1834
   b. The granting of the vote to the lower industrial working class with the Reform Bill of 1832
   c. The repeal of the Corn Law in 1846, which increased the price of bread for workers
   d. The reapportioning of voting districts along more equitable and reasonable lines

13. The 1848 revolution in France resulted in

   a. The continuation of Louis-Philippe's rule when he accepted liberal reforms
   b. New elections for the National Assembly, resulting in a victory for radical republicans
   c. Europe's first socialist state under the guidance of the workshops
   d. An authoritarian government ruled by Louis Napoleon

14. The student response in Germany to the French Revolution of 1848 was one of

   a. Outrage and calls for war against France
   b. Disbelief and despair over the coming chaos
   c. Enthusiasm and optimism that republican reforms would also come to Germany
   d. Joy that the French state was about to self-destruct

15. The social and political upheavals in central Europe through 1848-1849 led to

   a. The failure of the Frankfurt Assembly in Germany
   b. An independent state for Hungary
   c. A united German-Austrian state patterned on the dreams of the *Grossdeutsch*
   d. The continued dominance of Metternich in Austria

16. Young Italy was not

   a. Founded by Mazzini
   b. For a united Italian Republic
   c. Anti-Catholic
   d. A product of *risorgimento*

17. Compared to his counterparts in Paris and London, the Nineteenth Century Berlin police officer was better

    a.   Dressed, with a uniform designed for maneuvers and pleasant appearance
    b.   Paid, with full sick leave and retirement benefits
    c.   Armed, with a firearm that made him the equivalent of a soldier
    d.   Disciplined, with six weeks off each summer for further training

18. William Blake best summed up the Romantic view of science by

    a.   Calling for the creation of a new social order based on rationalism and technology
    b.   Writing the poem *Milton*, which called for ethics in science and more experimentation
    c.   Acknowledging that it was a necessary evil which would turn out to benefit mankind
    d.   Denouncing its proclaimed knowledge and accusing it of destroying human imagination

19. Romanticism was characterized by

    a.   Chateaubriand, whose paintings anticipated the Impressionist movement
    b.   Beethoven, whose dramatic compositions bridged the gap between classicism and Romanticism
    c.   Delacroix, who broke classical conventions by using only black and white in his paintings
    d.   Friedrich, whose "program" music played on the emotions of listeners

20. The Age of Romanticism witnessed

    a.   A Catholic revival, especially in Germany
    b.   Rejection by artist and musicians of all religious sensibilities
    c.   A Protestant numerical decline in Britain
    d.   The importation of Indian mysticism to Europe

Complete the Following Sentences:

1. At the Congress of Vienna, Austria was represented by _____, Britain _____, and France by _____.

2. The Napoleonic Era in Europe weakened Spanish control of the American colonies, and _____ _____, known as the Liberator, led Latin American armies of independence to victory. The American policy called the _____ _____ helped guarantee this independence.

3. By the Treaty of Adrianople, Turkey agreed to let _____, _____, and _____ decide the fate of Greece. They declared her _____.

4. After the _____ _____ against his accession, Russia's Nicholas I made his _____ _____ a spy organization with sweeping powers.

5. After the study of population growth by _____ _____ called into question the idea of human progress, the study of wages by _____ _____ held that governmental attempts to alter nature's iron laws were futile.

6. Charles Fourier advocated the establishment of voluntary economic communities called _____, and Robert Owen tried the idea in two places, successfully at _____ _____ in Scotland, unsuccessfully at _____ _____ in Indiana.

7. Flora Tristan advocated a utopian synthesis of socialism and _____ in which men and women would live in _____ _____.

8. The French Revolution of 1848 deposed the conservative king _____ and established a Second Republic under President _____ _____ _____.

9. The Metropolitan policemen of Paris, created under the leadership of Louis-Maurice _____, were called simply _____ and carried only a _____ by day and a _____ by night.

10. Romantic literature featured a range of subjects, from the Scottish historical novels of _____ _____ to the strange tale of *Frankenstein* by _____ _____.

Place the Following in Chronological Order and Give Dates:

1.   Repeal of Corn Laws in Britain   1.

2.   Decembrist Revolt in Russia   2.

3.   July Revolution in France   3.

4.   Beginning of Greek revolt against the Turks   4.

5.   British Reform Act   5.

6.   Revolts or revolutions in France, Germany, Italy, and Austria   6.

7.   Beginning of Wars of Independence in Latin America   7.

Questions for Critical Thought:

1.   Outline the Peace of Paris that emerged from the Congress of Vienna. How did it seek to establish a balance of power? Why is it called a Monument to Conservatism?

2.   Explain the ideology of nineteenth-century Conservatism, and show how it both dominated and provoked reaction during the period from 1815 to 1848.

3.   List all the revolts against the "Bourbon" monarchies between 1815-1848. What were their common causes, and what did they generally achieve?

4.   Compare and contrast the period 1815-1870 in Britain and in France. Account for the different set of events and final results.

5.   List the intellectual bases on which the various movements against Conservatism were mounted. Explain how each one contributed to the desire for and belief in change.

6.   Describe the Revolutions of 1848, where they occurred, who led them, what they hoped to achieve, and how each one ended.

7.   What effects did the Conservative Age have on daily life in Europe? What effects did the Liberal era that followed it have? In what sense were these two sides of a single coin?

8.   Define Romanticism. Discuss its characteristics, its major representatives, the various fields of the arts it affected, and what its lasting achievements were.

Analysis of Primary Source Documents:

1.   According to Austria's Prince Metternich, what characteristics of a nation give its people security and stability? Explain how each characteristic contributes to the whole.

2.   What did the German student of 1845 dream of accomplishing? How did he distinguish himself from his father's generation? How realistic were his goals?

3.   How do John Stuart Mill's views on "liberty" reflect the death of an old world and the birth of a new one? How will such ideas be tested in the next century?

4.   Explain in simplest terms Macauley's argument for the Reform Act of 1832. Show why he is considered one of the greatest of pragmatists.

5.   Describe the enthusiasm of young German liberals like Carl Schurz when their long-awaited revolution seemed at hand. Suggest three probable reactions among such young men when they realized it had failed.

6.   Outline the "doctrine" of nineteenth-century Nationalism as illustrated by the Young Italy Oath. How and to what degree was it, as some have argued, a secular religion?

7.   What complaints did London police of the 1840s have about their working conditions? How effectively did their petition communicate their complaints? Explain.

8.   Explain the Nineteenth Century's love for "Gothic" literature, particularly its tendency to combine romance and horror, as illustrated by the writings of Edgar Allen Poe. What does this say about the age—and the Romantic Movement?

AN AGE OF NATIONALISM AND REALISM (1850-1871)

Chapter Outline:

I. The France of Napoleon III
    A. Louis Napoleon as President
        1. Patience in Winning Support
        2. Election as Emperor
    B. The Second Napoleonic Empire
        1. Stimulating the Economy
        2. Rebuilding Paris
        3. Limiting Freedoms
        4. Napoleon's Opponents
        5. Foreign Policy and the Crimean War

II. National Unification Movements
    A. Italy
        1. The House of Savoy and Victor Emmanuel
        2. Camillo di Cavour
        3. Garibaldi and the Red Shirts
        4. Unification
    B. Germany
        1. William I Hohenzollern
        2. Otto von Bismarck and *Realpolitik*
        3. The Danish War (1864)
        4. The Austro-Prussian War (1866)
        5. The Franco-Prussian War (1870-1871)
        6. Unification

III. Nation Building and Reform: the National State at Mid-Century
    A. The Austrian Empire
        1. Francis Joseph and the Dual Monarchy
        2. Domination of Germans and Magyars

B. Imperial Russia
   1. Alexander II and the Emancipation of the Serfs
   2. The *Zemstvos* Assemblies
   3. Alexander Herzen and Populism
C. Britain's Victorian Age
   1. Palmerston's Chauvinism
   2. Disraeli and the Reform of 1867
   3. Gladstone and the Liberal Party
D. The United States
   1. Compromises of 1820 and 1850
   2. The Civil War and An End to Slavery
   3. Reunion of a Divided Nation
E. Canadian Nationhood

IV. Industrialization and the Marxist Response
  A. Industrialization of the Continent
    1. Less Barriers to International Trade
    2. Weak Trade Unions
  B. Marx and Marxism
    1. The Life and Experience of Karl Marx
    2. *The Communist Manifesto*
    3. Bourgeoisie and Proletariat
    4. The Classless Society

V. Science and Culture in An Age of Realism
  A. A New Age of Science
    1. Proliferation of Discoveries
    2. Faith in Science's Benefits
  B. Darwin and the Theory of Evolution
    1. Darwin's Trip on the *Beagle*
    2. "Natural Selection"
  C. A Revolution in Health Care
    1. Pasteur and Lister
    2. Women in Medicine
  D. Auguste Comte and Positivism
  E. Realism in Literature and Art
    1. The Realistic Novel
      a. Gustave Flaubert
      b. William Thackeray
      c. Charles Dickens

2. Realism in Art
   a. Gustave Courbet
   b. Jean-Francois Millet
F. Music: The Twilight of Romanticism
   1. Franz Liszt
   2. Richard Wagner

Chapter Summary:

After the midpoint of the Nineteenth Century, the suppressed emotions that had constantly bubbled for three decades finally erupted. The nations of Europe spent their energies in unification or reform; and the result affected Western development for the next century.

The memories of Napoleonic greatness which had haunted France saw fulfillment with first the election as president and then the proclamation as emperor of Napoleon's nephew, who took the grand title Emperor Napoleon III. From 1852 until he was deposed after France's defeat by Prussia in 1870, Napoleon made and unmade policy across the continent and even meddled in the affairs of the New World. The dreams of Mazzini were fulfilled when Cavour and Garibaldi, working sometimes at odds, succeeded in unifying Italy for the first time since the fall of the Roman Empire. Under the guidance of Bismarck, Prussia maneuvered and fought its way to the head of a unified German Empire. In Russia and the United States, serfs and slaves were freed, in the former by imperial decree, in the latter by constitutional amendment. And in Britain the pressures of industrialization forced a series of reforms that made the realm of Queen Victoria more democratic.

Science continued to make discoveries and to change life both socially and personally. Yet while health care greatly improved with discoveries about bacteria and infection, more and more workers fell into what Marx called the "wage slavery" of the industrial market. While political leaders like Disraeli and Gladstone believed that justice could be achieved by reform, Marx held that only a revolution of the workers would bring about a classless society. Both the *realpolitik* of nations and the realities of industrial life affected the arts, ushering in a new era of Realism. The world was often brutal and grim, and writers and artists portrayed it with pitiless accuracy.

Identify:

1. *Realpolitik*

2. Baron Haussmann

3. Sevastopol

4. Victor Emmanuel II

5. Red Shirts

6. Bismarck

7. *Reichstag*

8. Francis Joseph

9. *Ausgleich*

10. Alexander Herzen

11. Lord Palmerston

12. Missouri Compromise

13. Compromise of 1850

14. Karl Marx

15. *Das Kapital*

16. Ignaz Semmelweis

17. Harriet Hunt

18. Elizabeth Blackwell

19. Auguste Comte

20. William Thackeray

Match the Following Words with their Definitions:

1. Camillo di Cavour

2. Giuseppi Garibaldi

3. Benjamin Disraeli

4. William Gladstone

5. Dialectical Materialism

6. Michael Faraday

7. Louis Pasteur

8. Joseph Lister

9. Positivism

10. Gustave Flaubert

A. Conservative British prime minister who passed the Reform Bill of 1867

B. Karl Marx's explanation for the way economic forces will bring a classless society

C. Auguste Comte's theory that only scientifically verified facts are valid

D. Using carbolic acid, he eliminated surgical infections

E. Prime Minister of Piedmont who helped make Victor Emmanuel King of Italy

F. Builder of the first generator of electricity

G. Perfector of the realist novel with his *Madame Bovary*

H. Military leader who added Sicily to the new Kingdom of Italy

I. Chemist who pioneered in fermentation and bacteriology

J. Liberal British prime minister who introduced the secret ballot

Choose the Correct Answer:

1. In establishing the Second Empire, Napoleon III

    a. Received the overwhelming support of the people
    b. Granted the National Assembly stronger powers
    c. Rescinded universal male suffrage
    d. Cared little about public opinion

2. Under the "liberal empire" of Napoleon III in the 1860s

    a. Tariffs on foreign goods were lowered
    b. The Legislative Corps was permitted more say in affairs of state
    c. Trade unions and the right to strike were legalized
    d. All of the above

3. Napoleon III chose Baron Haussmann to rebuild

    a. The National Assembly
    b. Charlemagne's ancient capital of Aix-la-Chapelle
    c. The French Catholic Church
    d. The city of Paris

4. The Crimean War convinced Napoleon III that he had an international mission to

    a. Champion movements for national independence
    b. Conquer Europe for liberalism
    c. Referee continental disputes
    d. Contain the military ambitions of Russia

5. An overall result of the Crimean War was

    a. The reinforcement of the Concert of Europe until 1914
    b. Continued Russian expansionism into Europe for the next two decades
    c. Increased British involvement in continental affairs
    d. An international climate in which both Italian and German unification were possible

6. As leader of the Italian unification movement, Camillo di Cavour

    a. Had no preconceived plan for the unification
    b. Personally led Italian troops against Austria
    c. Supported Prussia against Austria with Italian troops in 1866
    d. Considered Napoleon III to be Italy's most bitter enemy

7. Before Otto von Bismarck, Prussia was characterized by

    a. A deteriorating army under William I
    b. A system of voting determined by wealth
    c. A resentful middle class with no say in the lower house of the legislature
    d. A parliament without power to reject the king's legislation

8. A result of Bismarck's Austro-Prussian War was

    a. Austria's annexation into the North German Confederation
    b. The reduction of Austria to a second-rate power
    c. Liberal Prussian condemnation of Bismarck's expansionist policies
    d. None of the above

9. The immediate cause of the Franco-Prussian War was

    a. The ascent of a French prince to the Spanish throne
    b. A Bismarck edited telegram from King William I
    c. The French invasion of Alsace-Lorraine
    d. Napoleon III's annexation of Schleswig-Holstein

10. The creation of the dual monarchy of Austria-Hungary

    a. Allowed Magyars and German-speaking Austrians to dominate ethnic minorities
    b. Enabled Alexander von Bach to become an absolute dictator
    c. Left Hungary independent in its domestic affairs
    d. Overturned the Compromise of 1867

11. Between 1810 and 1860, the United States was held together largely by

    a. A military force that suppressed violence in the cities
    b. The even distribution of industrial wealth
    c. A series of compromises over slavery
    d. The threat of a strong Mexico and Canada on the borders

12. Russia and the United States were similar in the 1860's in that both

    a. Experienced devastating civil wars
    b. Saw radical liberals assassinate high government officials
    c. Fought unsuccessful wars against Britain
    d. Emancipated enslaved populations within their borders

13. As British prime minister from 1855 to 1865, Lord Palmerston was responsible for

    a. Instituting universal male suffrage
    b. Chauvinistically defending British interests worldwide
    c. Defending the interests of the lower working class
    d. Opening civil service positions to competition

14. Industrialization of the Continent from 1850 to 1870 saw

    a. Germany and France surpass Britain in iron production
    b. The complete replacement of hand looms for power ones
    c. Railroads become the major area of industrial expansion
    d. Charcoal iron smelting replace coke-blast smelting

15. According to Karl Marx's vision for the industrial future, the state would

    a. Be violently destroyed with a class war
    b. Wither away because it would be unnecessary
    c. Dominate every part of the citizen's life
    d. Be made efficient through technological bureaucracy

16. The theoretical discoveries in science during the Nineteenth Century led to all of the following *except*

    a. A renewal of religious faith and spiritual commitment
    b. The acceptance of material reality as the only reality
    c. Great advances in mathematics and thermodynamics
    d. Technological advancements that affected everyone

17. Which of the following best applies to Charles Darwin and his evolutionary theory?

    a. It was based on the idea of "survival of the fittest," in which advantageous variants determine survival
    b. His *Origin of Species* traced man's evolution from animal to human
    c. His books were the first to promise a theory of evolution
    d. His ideas were accepted by religious communities because they held man in such high esteem

18. The first woman to earn a medical degree was

    a. Elizabeth Brown in England
    b. Elizabeth Blackwell in the United States
    c. Elizabeth McElroy in Scotland
    d. Elizabeth Baker in Ireland

19. In addition to portraying everyday life, the literary realists of the mid-Nineteenth Century were interested in

    a. Eschewing romantic imagery the way Dickens did
    b. Employing poetic and emotional language to bring about a move toward social reform
    c. Allowing their characters to speak for themselves
    d. Showing the positive values of middle-class life

20. Realist art of the Nineteenth Century was

    a. Praised by critics for showing the beauty of common people
    b. Characterized by urban scenes like those of Millet
    c. Recognized by its romantic sentimentality
    d. Particularly interested in the natural environment

Complete the Following Sentences:

1. With the disintegration of the _____ Empire, Russia tried to carve out a new sphere of influence, only to be attacked in its _____ Peninsula by France and _____, destroying the old _____ of Europe.

2. Garibaldi, a republican believer in Mazzini's _____ movement, was finally persuaded to accept an Italian kingdom under King _____ _____ of the house of _____.

3. In order to achieve German unification, Bismarck successfully went to war against _____, _____, and _____, the latter ending with the proclamation of the German _____.

4. Alexander II's Emancipation Edict allowed former Russian serfs to own _____, _____ as they chose, and bring lawsuits; but resentment against the limits of freedom led to Alexander's _____ in 1881.

5. Although the British Liberal Party led in calls for voting reform, the Reform Bill of 1867 was passed under the leadership of the Conservative prime minister _____. In the next election, the _____ Party won a huge victory.

6. Karl Marx, descended from a line of _____ _____, was raised in the _____ faith but was denied a professorship because of his _____.

7. Marx and Engels claimed in their _____ _____ that a class war would end with the complete victory of _____ over _____ and a _____ society.

8. Charles Darwin gathered data for his theory while on a scientific expedition to _____ America and the _____ Pacific aboard the H.M.S. _____ .

9. Flaubert's realist novel *Madame Bovary* tells of a provincial woman inspired by _____ stories to experiment with _____, only to end up a _____, still unrepentant.

10. Richard Wagner helped realize the nationalist dream of a truly _____ opera, using ancient myths to write his *Ring of the* _____ .

Place the Following in Chronological Order and Give Dates:

1. British Reform Act passed   1.

2. American Civil War ends   2.

3. Second Empire proclaimed in France   3.

4. Italy annexes Rome   4.

5. German Empire proclaimed   5.

6. Austro-Prussian War   6.

7. Russian Emancipation Edict   7.

Questions for Critical Thought:

1. Describe the Second French Empire. How did it come about, what were its domestic characteristics, what were its foreign policies, and how did it end?

2. Describe the unification of Italy. Show how men and historical circumstances cooperated to achieve the dream of *risorgimento*.

- 3. Explain how Bismarck accomplished the unification of Germany. What kind of legacy did he leave his people and nation?

4. Discuss the progress made during the second half of the Nineteenth Century by the nations already unified by 1850. Show how "the liberal agenda" fared in each one.

5. Explain the theories of Karl Marx. What circumstances, political and personal, led him to them? Why would they so strongly appeal to radical reformers?

6. What did the second age of scientific discovery add to human knowledge? Was it more "practical" than the earlier age? Explain.

7. Define the term "Realism" as applied to the literature and art of the late Nineteenth Century. Give examples of it, and show its legacy to our own day.

8. What progress was made in professional medicine in the late Nineteenth Century? How did women break into the profession? Give examples.

Analysis of Primary Source Documents:

1. Show how Louis Napoleon used the high ideal of national well-being to forward his goal of personal power. In what ways was he a model for twentieth-century dictators?

2. Describe the newspaper account of Garibaldi's walk through war-torn Palermo. Then write the story as a more modern reporter might tell it.

3. Explain how Bismarck "edited" his king's telegram from Ems to make the French feel they had been insulted. What was his purpose in doing this, and how well did he succeed?

4. Compare and contrast the emancipation proclamations of Tsar Alexander II and Abraham Lincoln. Which was the more thorough and why?

5. Having read Marx's description of the way we will arrive at the classless society, how would you judge Marx's opinion of man's nature?

6. Why did Darwin's theory of man's origins cause such a stir? What did Nineteenth Century Britons find offensive and attractive about it?

7. Describe the first use of ether in surgery. How do you account for our writer's hyperbole?

8. What made Charles Dickens' description of industrial Birmingham so powerful? What does his portrayal say about his own feelings on the subject?

Map Exercise 12: The Unification of Germany and Italy

Using various shades of pencil, color and label the following:

Pinpoint and label the following:

Germany

1.   Alsace
2.   Baden
3.   Bavaria
4.   East Prussia
5.   Hanover
6.   Hesse
7.   Lorraine
8.   Oldenburg
9.   Prussia
10. Schleswig-Holstein
11. West Prussia
12. Württemburg

Italy

1.   Lombardy
2.   Modena
3.   Papal States
4.   Parma
5.   Piedmont
6.   Romagna
7.   Sardinia
8.   Savoy
9.   Tuscany
10. Two Sicilies
11. Umbria
12. Venezia

Germany

1.   Berlin
2.   Breslau
3.   Frankfurt
4.   Hamburg
5.   Leipzig
6.   Munich
7.   Strassburg
8.   Trier
9.   Weimar

Italy

1.   Florence
2.   Genoa
3.   Milan
4.   Naples
5.   Palermo
6.   Rome
7.   Venice

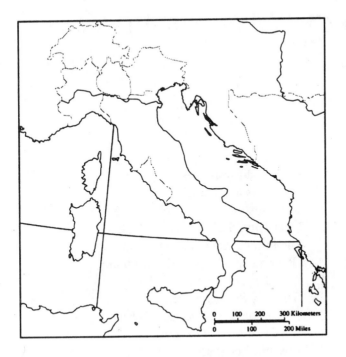

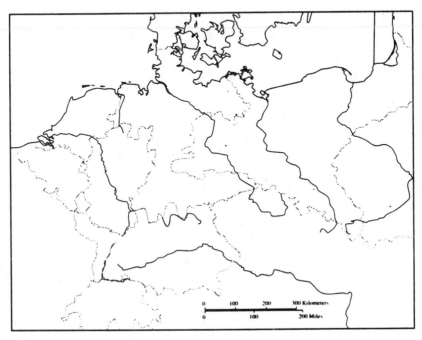

23 MASS SOCIETY IN AN "AGE OF PROGRESS" (1871-1894)

Chapter Outline:

I.   The Growth of Industrial Prosperity
    A.   New Products and New Markets
        1.   The Substitution of Steel for Iron
        2.   Electricity, the New Source of Energy
        3.   The Internal Combustion Engine
    B.   New Patterns in An Industrial Economy
        1.   From Depression to Prosperity
        2.   Germany Surpasses Britain
        3.   The Union of Science and Technology
        4.   The Creation of Two Europes
        5.   A World Economy
    C.   Women and New Job Opportunities
        1.   The Sweatshops
        2.   Office Work
        3.   An Increase in Prostitution
    D.   Organizing the Working Class
        1.   Socialist Parties
        2.   A Revision of Marxist Thought
            a.   Evolution, Not Revolution
            b.   The Divisiveness of Nationalism
        3.   The Role of Trade Unionism
        4.   The Anarchist Alternative

II.   The Emergence of Mass Society
    A.   Population Growth
        1.   Improved Public Sanitation
        2.   An Improved Diet
        3.   Increased Emigration

B. Transformation of the Urban Environment
   1. The Growth of Cities
   2. Improving Living Conditions
      a. Sanitation
      b. Housing
   3. Redesigning the Cities
C. The Social Structure of Mass Society
   1. The Elite: Wealth and Status
   2. The Middle Classes: Good Conduct
   3. The Lower Classes: Skilled, Semiskilled, Unskilled
D. The Role of Women
   1. The Cult of Domesticity
   2. Birth Control
   3. The Middle-Class Family
   4. The Working-Class Family
E. Education and Leisure in An Age of Mass Society
   1. Primary Education for All
      a. For A More Efficient Work Force
      b. For A More Intelligent Electorate
      c. A Demand for Teachers
      d. The Increase in Literacy
   2. Mass Leisure
      a. Dance Halls
      b. Tourism
      c. Sports

III. The National State
   A. Political Democracy in Western Europe
      1. British Reform
      2. France's Third Republic
      3. Parliamentary Government in Spain
      4. Italy's Instability
   B. Persistence of the Old Order in Central and Eastern Europe
      1. Germany: Bismarck's Conservatism
      2. Austria's Imperial Decrees
      3. Absolutism in Russia

Chapter Summary:

After 1871 the nations of Europe were preoccupied for a quarter century with achieving true national unity, adjusting to the economics of a second industrial revolution, and adapting to the realities of rapid urbanization. Despite the rise and acceleration of international rivalries and animosities, they were simply too busy to fight among themselves.

During this period inventions based on steel, electricity, and the internal combustion engine led to a new industrial economy which changed the nature of markets and created a true world economy. Women found new opportunities of work, yet also were seduced into a larger ring of subservience and prostitution. Socialist parties, with a more moderate form of Marxism, began organizing for action through trade unionism and political action. Europe suffered the birth pangs of a new age.

Mass Society was born. The European population increased dramatically through better sanitation and diet, yet emigration prevented overcrowding. Class divisions continued to dictate styles of living, and women of the upper strata were encouraged to pursue a cult of domesticity, yet this age also saw the dawn of female consciousness and of birth control. The amount and quality of education increased in order to provide a better-trained work force and a more intelligent voting public, and there arose more opportunities to enjoy life through leisure activities. The European Nations moved in two opposite directions. In Britain and France liberal parties increased democratic participation in government, while in Germany, Austria, and especially Russia, monarchs held to their powers with stubborn abandon. The times were changing, but it was not clear what the looming new century would bring.

Identify:

1. "Day-Trippers"

2. Guglielmo Marconi

3. Gottlieb Daimler

4. August Bebel

5. Eduard Bernstein

6. May Day

7. Michael Bakunin

8. Solomon Neumann

9. V.A. Huber

10. Port Sunlight

11. Consuelo Vanderbilt

12. Aletta Jacob

13. Guides

14. Barbara Bodichon

15. *Family Herald*

16. Rugby Union

17. Georges Boulanger

18. *Kulturkampf*

19. William II

20. Nicholas II

Match the Following Words with their Definitions:

1. Rudolf Virchow

2. Octavia Hill

3. Bertha Krupp

4. Consuelo Vanderbilt

5. Agnes Baden-Powell

6. Barbara Bodichon

7. Thomas Cook

8. William Gladstone

9. Commune

10. *Kulturkampf*

A. British founder of the Guides

B. Organizer of Temperance trips

C. Wealthiest woman in Germany at the turn of this century

D. Violently crushed in 1871

E. American who married into British royalty

F. Advocate of urban sanitation reform

G. Failed in an attempt to limit Catholic power

H. Pioneer in the field of female education

I. Worked to provide homes for the poor

J. Advocate of Irish Home Rule

Choose the Correct Answer:

1. Which of the following statements is false?

    a. Henry Ford produced the first light engine in 1886
    b. Marconi sent the first radio waves across the Atlantic in 1901
    c. Alexander Graham Bell invented the telephone in 1876
    d. Joseph Swan invented the light bulb

2. Cartels were designed primarily to

    a. Enrich nation states
    b. Raise funds for social programs
    c. Restrain competition that lowers prices
    d. Provide police protection for companies

3. Working-class men used which argument to try to keep women out of industrial work?

    a. That keeping them at home made for stronger families
    b. That they were physically too weak to do the work
    c. That it was not God's will for them to work
    d. That they were too politically active

4. Most large-city prostitutes were

    a. Wives bringing in extra money for their families
    b. Dead by the age of 30 from disease
    c. Held up for public ridicule in a church at least once in their careers
    d. Active for only a short time and went on to other work or marriage

5. Edward Bernstein stressed the need for

    a. Violent overthrow of capitalist governments
    b. Extermination of individualists
    c. Working within the political system to achieve socialism
    d. A literal faithfulness to every Marxist theory

6. Annual emigration from Europe to America

    a. More than doubled from 1880 to 1900
    b. Leveled off after 1890
    c. Had no positive benefits to European society
    d. Contained almost no Jews

7. The most successful legislative acts concerning public health

    a. Were passed in Russia
    b. Created boards of health that fought for reforms
    c. Seemed always to create more problems than they solved
    d. Were condemned by church officials as socialistic

8. Octavia Hill's housing venture was designed to

    a. Give the poor an environment in which to improve themselves
    b. Give charity to the helpless and hopeless poor
    c. Let the wealthy experience poverty for a week each year
    d. Break down class barriers

9. Experiments in public housing proved that

    a. Government housing was doomed to failure
    b. Poor people would not keep their premises sanitary
    c. Every project needed private monies to keep them afloat
    d. Governments must construct houses on a grand scale

10. An example of the way new industrial wealth combined with old aristocracy was the marriage of the Duke of Marlborough to

    a. The Italian Tia Ferrari
    b. The American Wallis Warfield Simpson
    c. The American Consuelo Vanderbilt
    d. The German Bertha Krupp

11. The wealthy elite of the new industrial age

    a. Came to be dominated by upper-middle-class families with fortunes made in industry
    b. Consisted mostly of landed aristocracy
    c. Controlled only slightly more total wealth than did all the working class
    d. Was more open to admission by newcomers in Russia than in any other country

12. In 1882, Dr. Aletta Jacob opened in Amsterdam Europe's first

    a. Housing unit for female industrial workers
    b. Birth control clinic
    c. Abortion clinic
    d. Home for unwed mothers

13. The middle classes of late nineteenth-century Europe

    a. Were composed of shopkeepers and manufacturers who barely lived above the property line
    b. Offered almost no opportunity for their women to improve themselves
    c. Were extremely concerned with propriety and adhered to values of hard work and Christian morality
    d. Viewed the idea of progress with extreme distrust

14. The domestic ideal of the late nineteenth-century middle-class family was

    a.   Each member holding a job so as to increase family income
    b.   Spending time together, especially at leisure activities
    c.   A strict, almost military command by the father
    d.   For boys only to be educated and girls to be married as early as possible

15. Changes in the standard of living from 1890 to 1914 affected the working-class family

    a.   Positively because with more children working the family income increased
    b.   Negligibly because most families could still not afford consumer products
    c.   Negatively because real income were severely reduced
    d.   Positively because working-class mothers could devote more time to child rearing

16. The motive for mass education is believed to have been political because

    a.   The expansion of voting rights demanded a more enlightened electorate
    b.   Politicians could win votes by promising more money for education
    c.   Contractors who built school buildings had political clout
    d.   The schools specialized in training government officials

17. Music and dance hall were obviously designed and operated for

    a.   An upper-class audience who liked to "slum" in poor neighborhoods
    b.   The soldiers from nearby barracks
    c.   An audience chiefly lower class and male
    d.   The benefit of theaters, which drew their talent from such training grounds

18. The Second French Empire was at last replaced by a

    a.   Restored monarchy, the "only true French regime"
    b.   Third Empire, under Napoleon IV
    c.   Communist regime, allied with Soviet Russia
    d.   Third Republic, which survived despite internal divisions

19. Which statement best applies to Germany under the chancellorship of Otto von Bismarck?

    a.   Prussia lost much of its leadership role in the military
    b.   Bismarck used coalitions until they accomplished their purposes, then dropped them
    c.   The Barmy stamped out almost all vestiges of civilian socialism
    d.   All regional differences disappeared under Bismarck's conciliatory hand

20. Which of these statements best applies to the Dual Monarchy of Austria-Hungary?

    a.   Both Austria and Hungary had parliamentary systems
    b.   The Magyars dominated the empire while William II reigned
    c.   The nationality problem remained unsolved and contributed to a strong German movement
    d.   Prime Minister Count Edward von Taafe was ousted in 1893 by Slavic minorities for failing to satisfy their demands

Complete the Following Sentences:

1. British industrialists fell behind Germans because they were suspicious of _____ and failed to invest in _____ schools.

2. Women first broke into the labor force because of the increased need for _____ _____ work, all of which required few skills beyond literacy except _____ and _____.

3. French socialism differed from socialism in other countries because it looked not to _____ but to the _____ _____ for justification.

4. Rapid urbanization meant that while in 1800 there were _____ European cities over 100,000 in population, by 1900 there were _____. During the same time period England's urban population went from _____ to _____ percent.

5. In England _____ and _____ were the first cities to have town councils build public housing, concluding that _____ _____ could not do all that was needed for the working classes.

6. Even though vulcanized rubber made possible the manufacture of _____ and _____ by 1850, they were not widely used for birth control until much later.

7. Liberals hoped that mass education would provide _____ and _____ training based on _____ values.

8. The independent Parisian republic called the _____ was ended when 20,000 people were _____ and 10,000 shipped to a _____ _____.

9. The _____ officers of the German army believed it their duty to defend _____ and _____; and their general staff answered only to the _____.

10. The paranoid Russian Emperor Alexander III greatly expanded the powers of his
_____ _____ and placed entire districts under _____
_____.

Place the Following in Chronological Order and Give Dates:

1. Bismarck's antisocialist law   1.

2. Bernstein's *Evolutionary Socialism* published   2.

3. Irish Land Act passed by British Parliament   3.

4. The new Spanish constitution   4.

5. The Paris Commune   5.

6. Aletta Jacob opens her clinic in Amsterdam   6.

7. British Housing Act passed   7.

Questions for Critical Thought:

1. How did the new industrial economy after 1871 differ from the previous industrial economy? What caused the changes?

2. Explain and describe the rise of socialism in its various forms after 1870. What caused its diffusion, and what were its attractions?

3. Describe the urbanization of Europe in the late Nineteenth Century, and how it both created problems and solved them.

4. Outline the class structure that developed in the new urban industrial society. How was it like and unlike earlier structures? What were its strengths and weaknesses?

5. What were the various roles of women in the new social structure? Did women live better or worse lives than in previous times?

6. Why and how did urban industrialism increase emphasis on education and leisure? How do we still see these effects?

7. Compare the democracies of Britain and France. How did each nation's history contribute to these developments?

8. What form did the new German state take? What is Bismarck's role in its formation?

9. How does Russia's history at the old century's end explain its violent history in the century to come?

Analysis of Primary Source Documents:

1. Explain why department stores proved so successful. What needs did they satisfy, and what sound economic principles did they follow?

2. What arguments did Edward Bernstein have with the Marxist view of history? To what extent was he still really a Marxist?

3. Using Octavia Hill as your example, show how early reformers combined compassion for the poor with shrewd business senses.

4. Give the response one of today's feminists might make to Elizabeth Poole Sanford's advice to women.

5. What moral values are celebrated in the H.B. Tristam fight song? What kind of men does English public school football want to produce?

6. According to the account left to us by Louise Michel, what was the purpose of the Paris Commune uprising, and what did it achieve?

7. To what extent was Bismarck, by trying to eliminate Socialist influence, forced to become a Socialist? How did his motives for social welfare differ from that of the Socialists?

Map Exercise 13: Europe in 1871

Using various shades of pencil, color and label the following:

1. Algeria
2. Austria-Hungary
3. Austria
4. Belgium
5. Bessarabia
6. Black Sea
7. Bosnia
8. Crimea
9. Croatia-Slovenia
10. Cyprus
11. Denmark
12. Finland
13. France
14. German Empire
15. Great Britain
16. Greece
17. Hungary
18. Italy
19. Luxemburg
20. Montenegro
21. Morocco
22. Netherlands
23. Norway and Sweden
24. Ottoman Empire
25. Poland
26. Portugal
27. Romania
28. Russian Empire
29. Serbia
30. Spain
31. Switzerland
32. Tunisia

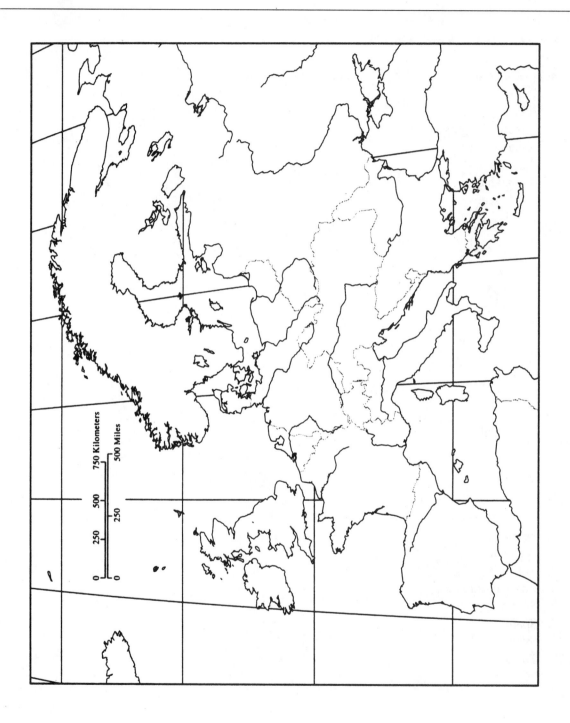

750 Kilometers

500 Miles

500

250

250

250

0

0

AN AGE OF MODERNITY AND ANXIETY (1894-1914)

Chapter Outline:

I. Toward the Modern Consciousness: Intellectual and Cultural Developments
   A. The Emergence of a New Physics
      1. Max Planck and Quanta
      2. Albert Einstein and Relativity
   B. Toward a New Understanding of the Irrational
      1. Friedrich Nietzsche and Superman
      2. Henri Bergson and the "Life Force"
      3. Georges Sorel
   C. Sigmund Freud and Pyschoanalysis
      1. The Unconscious
      2. Repression
   D. Social Darwinism and Racism
      1. Herbert Spencer's *Social Statistics*
      2. Friedrich von Bernhardi's Nationalism: The *Volk*
   E. Attack on Christianity and Church Responses
      1. Ernst Renan's *Life of Jesus*
      2. Pius IX and Leo X
      3. William Booth and the Salvation Army
   F. The Culture of Modernity
      1. Literature
         a. Emile Zola's Naturalism
         b. Tolstoy and Dostoevsky
         c. Yeats, Rilke, and Symbolism
      2. Art
         a. Pissarro, Morisot, Monet, and Impressionism
         b. Cezanne, Van Gogh, and Post-Impressionism
         c. Picasso, Kandinsky, and Abstraction

   3. Music
      a. Debussy's Impressionism
      b. Stravinsky's Primitivism

II.   Politics: New Directions and New Uncertainties
   A. The Women's Rights Movement
      1. Custody and Property
      2. Suffrage
      3. The New Woman
   B. Jews and Nationalism
      1. Christian Socialism's Racism
      2. Theodor Herzl and Zionism
   C. Liberalism Transformed
      1. Britain's Labor Party
      2. Italy's Corruption
   D. Growing Tensions in Germany
   E. Imperial Russia
      1. Industrialization and Socialism
      2. The Revolution of 1905
   F. The Progressive Age of the United States

III. The New Imperialism
   A. Causes
      1. Competition Among European Nations
      2. Social Darwinism and Racism
      3. Humanitarianism and Missions
      4. Economic Gain
   B. The Creation of Empires
      1. Africa
         a. Cape Colony and the Boer War
         b. Cecil Rhodes and British Strength
         c. The Scramble to Carve the Continent
      2. Asia
         a. James Cook and Australia
         b. China and the "Open Door"
         c. Matthew Perry and Japan
         d. The Pacific Islands
   C. Asian Responses to Imperialism
      1. Boxers and a Chinese Republic
      2. Meiji Modernization of Japan
      3. British Control of India

IV. International Rivalry and the Coming of War
    A. The Bismarckian System of Alliances
    B. New Directions and New Crises
       1. Triple Alliance and Triple Entente
       2. Crisis in the Balkans

Chapter Summary:

The period from 1894 to 1914 saw Europe expand its horizons, both in the rise of daring, new intellectual and cultural developments at home and in the creation of new empires abroad.

At home scientists were working on physical theories that would in time relegate the old Newtonian world to the past and usher in a much more insecure and dangerous world. Sigmund Freud concluded that man operates at the direction of unconscious motivations. The teachings of Charles Darwin were applied to society and used to justify racism and imperialism by saying that in the struggle of races and nations the fittest survive and make the world a better place. Christianity did constant battle with forces that threatened it. Modern forms began to appear in literature, the arts, and music.

The old empires in America and India had long either been lost or integrated into the European system when the Western nations began a second round of modern empire building toward the end of the Nineteenth Century. In a quarter century almost all of Africa was carved up and portioned out to be colonies of European nations; and in that same period Asia as well was divided into spheres of influence and trade. While the two old established Asian nations remained independent, China and Japan were also deeply affected and changed by Western imperialism. China was opened to trade and to Western concessions, leading to a violent native rebellion and to a revolution that toppled the Manchu Dynasty and established a Chinese republic. Japan opened up to the modern world to the extent that it adopted Western military, educational, governmental, and financial ways, even to the extent of taking colonies of its own in China and Korea.

Amid this ferment and expansionism the clouds of war were gathering. The great nations of Europe, competing with and fearing each other, formed defensive alliances with friends against foes and stockpiled weapons for a conflict that seemed to be more inevitable by the certainty of combatants that it could not be avoided.

Identify:

1. Quanta

2. Relativity

3. Superman

4. "Life force"

5. Repression

6. *Volk*

7. Pius IX

8. Leo XIII

9. Naturalism

10. Impressionism

11. Post-Impressionism

12. Primitivism

13. Christian Socialism

14. Zionism

15. Peter Stolypin

16. Imperialism

17. Great Trek

18. Rhodesia

19. "Open Door"

20. Meiji

Match the Following Words with their Definitions:

1. Herbert Spencer

2. Ernst Renan

3. Vasily Kandinsky

4. Igor Stravinsky

5. Boers

6. Cecil Rhodes

7. James Cook

8. Manchus

9. Boxers

10. Meiji

A. British captain who first explored Australia

B. Anti-foreign movement in turn-of-the-century China

C. Government that transformed Japan into a modern nation

D. Abstract expressionist who led flight from "visual reality"

E. Descendants of Dutch emigrants to southern Africa

F. Composer of the revolutionary *Rite of Spring*

G. Most prominent exponent of Social Darwinism

H. Diamond merchant who tried to overthrow the government of the South African Republic

I. Catholic who described Jesus not as the son of God but as a man

J. Last dynastic house of China, overthrown in 1912

Choose the Correct Answer:

1. Max Planck's discovery of "quanta" energy

    a. Brought Newtonian physics into serious question
    b. Proved that atoms radiate energy in a steady stream
    c. Reaffirmed the belief that science accurately describes reality
    d. Led to massive demonstrations in Russia

2. The actual literary creator of Superman was

    a. Henry Bergson
    b. Friedrich Nietzsche
    c. Sigmund Freud
    d. Albert Einstein

3. Albert Einstein

    a. Worked with Max Planck to develop the quantum theory
    b. Was from the first welcomed into the European scientific community
    c. Developed a theory in which neither time nor space exists independent of human experience
    d. Maintained the Newtonian scheme of the universe as one with absolute time and space

4. Sigmund Freud believed that the way to solve the conflicts of his psychologically disturbed patients was to

    a. Trace repression back to its childhood origins
    b. Use electrotherapy along with drugs
    c. Help them override the pleasure principle
    d. Destroy their superegos

5. Exponents of Social Darwinism in the late Nineteenth Century called for

    a. International struggle to establish what peoples are fittest to survive
    b. Communist expansion as the only way to help those who are economically weak
    c. A moratorium on war in order to save mankind from destruction
    d. National medical care programs for those unable to pay for it themselves

6. The German concept of the *Volk*

    a. Proclaimed that German culture is the world's highest
    b. Led to the belief that the Jews were out to destroy the Aryan race
    c. Represented the direction Social Darwinism took in that country
    d. All of the above

7. The growing challenges to the Christian churches from science and modern thought resulted in

    a. Harsh criticism of socialism and modernization by Pope Leo XIII in his *De Rerum Novarum*
    b. Admission of Catholic shortcomings by Pope Pius IX in his *Syllabus of Errors*
    c. A portrait of Jesus as a non-divine person by Ernst Renan in his *Life of Jesus*
    d. The adoption of the religious ideals of Modernism both by Protestants and Catholics

8. Zola's literary Naturalism was deeply influenced by

    a. Freud's theory of the Unconscious
    b. Herzl's call for a Jewish state
    c. Darwin's theory of the struggle for survival
    d. Nietzsche's call for a superman

9. Dostoevsky's life experiences led him to believe that

    a. By devotion to socialism the world could be saved
    b. Russia needed a Japanese form of emperor worship
    c. The Church must revert to poverty in order to be Christ-like
    d. Through suffering the soul is purified

10. The early feminist movement was known for

    a. Sharing identical goals with the trade union movement
    b. Achievements in nursing by Nightingale and Sieveking
    c. Iconoclastic speeches by the German leader Millicent Fawcett
    d. Achieving woman suffrage across Europe by 1914

11. The first recorded martyr to the cause of women's suffrage was

    a. Millicent Fawcett, starved by prison guards
    b. Emily Davison, trampled by a horse
    c. Carol Crowe, poisoned by male laborers
    d. Emmeline Pankhurst, drowned by water from fire hoses

12. Theodor Herzl's *Jewish State* concluded that

    a. Jews should remain in Europe and wait for the tide of anti-Semitism to turn
    b. The Zionist movement was a Utopian dream that should best be abandoned
    c. The creation of a Jewish nation in Palestine was both feasible and advisable
    d. A separate Jewish homeland would never be tolerated by the European nations

13. Imperialism in the late Nineteenth Century was usually justified by European masters as

    a. Necessary to maintain international prestige
    b. A moral responsibility of Europeans to bring civilization to other peoples
    c. Part of the natural order of Social Darwinism
    d. All of the above

14. European imperialism in Africa was best characterized by

    a.   Grossly mismatched battles in which Europeans easily defeated native resistance
    b.   The domination of North Africa by the Germans
    c.   Rivalries between European powers leading to full-scale wars on the African continent
    d.   Cooperative and equitable agreements between Europeans and native Africans

15. The Englishman who carved out an African colony of his own was

    a.   Henry Stanley
    b.   Cecil Rhodes
    c.   David Livingstone
    d.   Jan Smuts

16. Which of the following statements best applies to European imperialism in Asia?

    a.   Russia showed little interest in Asia until 1918
    b.   The British acquired the Philippines in a war with Spain
    c.   China was divided by the great powers in spheres of influence
    d.   The United States dominated southeast Asia after 1895

17. Choose the correct relationship between the Asian nation and its response to European imperialism

    a.   China—the educated classes entered British civil service, but they continued to be resentful
    b.   India—anti-foreign violence broke out in the Boxer Rebellion and resulted in harsher colonial rule
    c.   Japan—rapidly adopted Western military and industrial techniques in order to become an imperial power itself
    d.   Philippines—won independence from the British with a series of raids on Manilla

18. Meiji Japan imitated

    a.   The U.S. in military and Germany in industrial matters
    b.   France in military and Britain in industrial matters
    c.   Britain in military and France in industrial matters
    d.   Germany in military and the U.S. in industrial matters

19. Nineteenth-century British rule in India witnessed

   a. Educated Indians achieve high positions in the civil service
   b. An organized independence movement threaten British rule
   c. The destruction of the countryside due to a series of internal wars
   d. The bulk of the native population remain illiterate and malnourished

20. Following the dismissal of Bismarck by William II in 1890, Germany

   a. Became increasingly active in foreign affairs, pursuing its "place in the sun"
   b. Became ever more closely allied with Britain
   c. Abandoned plans for building a navy and concentrated fully on building its army
   d. Succeeded in splitting the Entente Cordiale agreed to by Britain and France

Complete the Following Sentences:

1. Max Planck concluded that bodies radiate energy in irregular packets called _____, thus creating questions about the old view of _____ and the physics of _____ _____.

2. Einstein's special theory of _____ said space and time are not absolute but depend upon the _____, and he elaborated that if matter disappeared, so too would _____ and _____.

3. Freud taught that human behavior is largely affected by the _____, former experiences of which we are _____, but which often appear in coded form in _____.

4. Friedrich von Bernhardi added to the theory of Social _____ the claim that _____, a _____ necessity, is "the father of all things."

5. Pope Leo XIII upheld the right of private _____ yet criticized "naked" _____; and he called Christian much that was in _____ while condemning _____ for being materialistic and antireligious.

6. Pissarro and Monet painted nature directly, seeking to capture the first _____ and to show the changing effects of _____ on nature, thus laying the foundations for _____ painting.

7. The "new imperialism" of the late Nineteenth Century involved European domination of _____ and _____, two areas largely ignored earlier. It also involved deeper _____ into non-European societies.

8. The Boers made their Great Trek and set up governments in the _____ and the _____ _____ _____ in order to avoid _____ rule.

9. Although the Society of Harmonious Fists, known as _____, tried to free China from foreign control, other revolutionaries, led by _____ _____, worked to overthrow the _____ dynasty.

10. Emperor Mutsuhito of Japan, calling his reign the _____, sought to transform his society by reform and conquest, claiming territory on the _____ mainland and annexing _____ after defeating _____ in 1905.

Place the Following in Chronological Order and Give Dates:

1. Boxer Rebellion in China   1.

2. Three Emperors' League formed   2.

3. British take Hong Kong   3.

4. Japan annexes Korea   4.

5. Victoria crowned Empress of India 5.

6. Suez Canal opened   6.

7. Triple Entente formed   7.

Questions for Critical Thought:

1. What new ideas came into the world of science—particularly physics and psychology—at the turn of the Twentieth Century? Why did they meet with an "irrational" response from philosophers?

2. How did Freud's analysis of human nature depart from previous analyses? To what extent did Freudian analysis become "the future" of anthropology?

3. Explain Social Darwinism, and show how it helped give direction and legitimacy to a new wave of racism. What were Jewish responses to the related phenomenon of anti-Semitism?

4. Describe turn-of-the-century "attacks" on organized Christianity, and show how the churches responded to what they saw as threats.

5. Discuss the various forms that turn-of-the-century art, architecture, and literature took. Give an overall explanation for these movements. Where did the arts seem headed in 1914?

6. How and why did the feminist movement come about? In what ways was it a product of its times?

7. Describe the "New Imperialism" of the late Nineteenth Century . How was it different from the earlier imperialism? What were its causes and results?

8. How did Europe's Asian and African empires differ? Why? What were the reactions of already established nations in each continent to these empires?

9. Describe the system of alliances that both held off war until 1914 and then helped bring it on. What brought the long European peace to an end?

Analysis of Primary Source Documents:

1. What do you learn of Freud's methodology by reading his lecture on repression? What explanation do you find here for the immense prestige he gained in his own lifetime?

2. Read aloud, then describe the "feeling" Rimbaud's poem gives you. In what sense does he give "meaning without meaning" to a reader?

3. How would a typical woman of 1879 have felt watching Ibsen's *A Doll's House*? What might "Nora" have said to such women had she turned to address the audience directly?

4. What parts of Theodor Herzl's proposal for a Jewish homeland came true, and what parts did not? How different is today's nation of Israel from Herzl's dream?

5. Show how the petition brought to Nicholas II in 1905 indicates that the petitioners were or were not a threat to peace. What does their massacre say about the emperor and Russian state at that time?

6. What was Kipling's "white man's burden," how were white men to bear it, and what would be their reward?

7. Using Morel's *Black Man's Burden*, explain the damage colonialism did to African people, their society, and their culture.

8. In his 1908 interview with the British *Daily Telegraph*, Kaiser William II spoke his mind. What did he mean to say, and how did he end up saying it? How do you account for the difference?

Map Exercise 14: Africa in 1914

Using various shades of pencil, color and label the following:

1. Algeria
2. Angola
3. Atlantic Ocean
4. Basutoland
5. Cameroon
6. Congo
7. Egypt
8. Eritrea
9. Ethiopia
10. German East Africa
11. Guinea
12. Indian Ocean
13. Kenya
14. Liberia
15. Libya
16. Madagascar
17. Mediterranean Sea
18. Morocco
19. Mozambique
20. Nigeria
21. Red Sea
22. Rio de Oro
23. Senegal
24. Sierra Leone
25. Somaliland
26. South Africa
27. South West Africa
28. Swaziland
29. Tunis
39. Uganda
31. West Africa

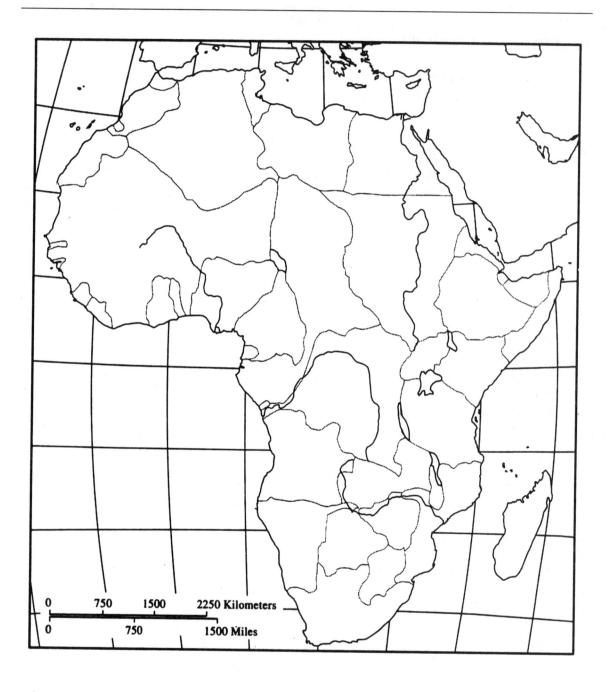

0   750   1500   2250 Kilometers

0   750   1500 Miles

CHAPTER

THE BEGINNING OF THE TWENTIETH-CENTURY CRISIS: WAR AND REVOLUTION

25

Chapter Outline:

D. The Impact of Total War on the Home Front
    1. Political Centralization and Economic Regulation
    2. Public Order and Public Opinion
        a. The Irish Uprising
        b. Army Mutinies
    3. Social Impact of Total War
        a. Benefits to Labor
        b. New Roles for Women
        c. Challenges to Class
        d. Inflation

III. War and Revolution
    A. The Russian Revolution
        1. March Revolution and a Provisional Government
        2. Lenin and the Bolshevik (October) Revolution
        3. The Treaty of Brest-Litovsk
        4. Civil War
    B. The Last Year of the War: 1918
        1. Germany's Last Gamble
        2. Armistice: November 11
    C. Revolutions in Germany and Austria
        1. The New German Republic
        2. The Division of the Austrian Empire

IV. The Paris Peace Settlement
    A. The Big Four
        1. Wilson's Ideals: The Fourteen Points
        2. The Quest for Reward and Retribution
    B. The Treaty of Versailles
        1. Dismemberment of Empires
        2. A Failure of Vision
        3. The League of Nations
        4. America's New Isolationism
        5. The End of European Hegemony

Chapter Summary:

The Twentieth Century really began not in 1900 but with the outbreak of World War I in 1914. The Great War, as it was called until a second world war broke out in 1939, ended the military alliances and styles of the life left over from the century past and ushered in the new world of a truly new century.

In the summer of 1914, Archduke Francis Ferdinand of Austria-Hungary was assassinated in the Bosnian capital of Sarajevo, and within six weeks the major nations of Europe were at war with each other in accordance with their myriad treaties, many of them until that time kept secret. For over a quarter of a century the growth of nationalistic competition had combined with an equally dangerous growth in military weaponry all across the continent to make Europe a powder keg waiting to burst into flame. The assassination was but the spark that brought ignition.

Since Germany had no trouble defeating Russian armies, it became evident quite early in the conflict that the war would be won and lost on the Western Front, between Germany and the Allies, Britain and France. Yet the war dragged on for four long years, much of it fought from trenches, as morale dropped lower and lower. Unrest spread through both camps and at home, where the belligerents had to keep their civilian populations in line with unusually harsh measures. Only in Russia did the government lose control; and there the Tsar and his family were murdered, ushering in a new regime. Out of the chaos that followed the March Revolution, Lenin's Bolshevik Party finally emerged triumphant. Russia would be a Communist state for over seventy years.

When the war eventually ended, the two losers experienced the revolutions that had threatened them during the war; and both Germany and Austria became republics. The victors met in Paris to make the peace and themselves could not agree on whether to establish a new and just world order or punish the Germans. Eventually they created an order that virtually assured that there would be another world war in the future.

Identify:

1. Balkans

2. Black Hand

3. Schlieffen Plan

4. Joseph Joffre

5. Gallipoli

6. Easter Rebellion

7. DORA

8. Hemophilia

9. Provisional Government

10. Mensheviks

11. Bolsheviks

12. Lenin

13. Brest-Litovsk

14. Trotsky

15. Red Terror

16. Rosa Luxemburg

17. Fourteen Points

18. Reparations

19. War Guilt Clause

20. John Maynard Keynes

Match the Following Words with their Definitions:

1. Alfred von Schlieffen

2. Paul von Hindenburg

3. Lusitania

4. DORA

5. Rasputin

6. April Theses

7. Brest-Litovsk

8. Cheka

9. Friedrich Ebert

10. Georges Clemenceau

A. Gave permission for Britain to arrest war dissenters as traitors

B. Lenin's plan of the Bolshevik revolution

C. Bolshevik secret police

D. Commander of first victories in World War I

E. Site of Russian-German peace conference

F. Leader of effort to punish Germany for its war acts

G. British ship sunk in 1915 with the loss of 100 American lives

H. Socialist leader of the new German republic of 1918

I. "Holy man" assassinated in 1916

J. Author of the two-front plan for fighting in World War I

Choose the Correct Answer:

1. Before the outbreak of World War I in 1914, the outlook on the future by most Europeans was

    a. Highly optimistic, expecting material progress and an "earthly paradise"
    b. One of extreme indifference to the future and a pursuit of recklessness
    c. Extremely negative, believing the end of the world was probably near
    d. Completely dependent on the good graces of socialistic governments

2. The rivalry between which two states for domination of southeastern Europe helped create serious tensions just before World War I?

    a. Germany and Italy
    b. Russia and Italy
    c. Austria-Hungary and Russia
    d. Britain and France

3. The immediate cause of the start of World War I was

    a. An uprising of peasants in Catholic Bavaria
    b. The assassination of Archduke Francis Ferdinand
    c. The German invasion of Poland
    d. A German naval blockade of Britain

4. In August, 1914, most observers and participants believed that the war would

    a. Be the dawn of a Communist Age
    b. Redeem Europe by ending selfishness
    c. Mark the end of Western civilization
    d. In the long term revive Europe's economy

5. The most important consequence of the first year in World War I was

    a. Stalemate on the Western Front after the First Battle of the Marne
    b. Italy's fateful decision to switch over to the German and Austrian side
    c. The collapse of the German army on the Russian Front
    d. Serbia's success in battles with Austria

6. The British officer who incited Arab princes to rebel against their Turkish overlords was

    a. Bill Slim
    b. Charles Mountbatten
    c. Ray Hamilton
    d. T.E. Lawrence

7. Trench warfare on the Western Front was characterized by

    a. Quick advances and seizures of land back and forth
    b. Few casualties because of the good fortifications
    c. Dreary boredom and static routines
    d. High morale and assurance of victory by both sides

8. Before he became the British prime minister, David Lloyd George served his government as Minister of

    a. Munitions
    b. Labour
    c. Finance
    d. Foreign Affairs

9.   As the war expanded from Europe

   a.   Britain wiped out the Turks in Africa
   b.   Germany used its colonies to wage war worldwide
   c.   Italy played a leading role against new allies rushing to the side of the Central Powers
   d.   China played a key role in Asia

10.   The United States finally decided to enter the war because of

   a.   A surprise German invasion of Mexico
   b.   Germany's refusal to stop unrestricted submarine warfare
   c.   President Wilson's dream of an American Empire
   d.   The assassination of the American ambassador in Vienna

11.   The entry of the United States into World War I

   a.   Gave the Allies a much needed psychological boost
   b.   Made the German Naval Staff suggest surrender
   c.   Was in response to Turkey's entrance on the side of Germany
   d.   Put an end to Germany's use of submarine warfare

12.   As public morale weakened in the later stages of the war

   a.   Workers' strikes lessened because of brutal suppression
   b.   Clemenceau's liberal French government let internal dissent dictate government policy
   c.   Propaganda posters lost all meaning and were abandoned
   d.   Police powers were expanded to include the arrest of dissenters as traitors

13.   Women hired for wartime work generally believed their jobs were

   a.   Critical to the war effort
   b.   Tasks men could do much better if they were available
   c.   Temporary and would end with the war
   d.   Patriotic obligations, fully as important as battle

14.   The most visible effect of World War I on European society was

   a.   An end to unemployment
   b.   An end to street crime
   c.   A dramatic increase in church attendance
   d.   A new positive outlook by young people

15. Which of the following best describes the wartime Russian government?

    a.   Holy man Rasputin ran the bureaucracy efficiently
    b.   The Tsarina Alexandra kept Nicholas ignorant of domestic problems
    c.   The general population was supportive throughout the war
    d.   Numerous reforms kept the peasants happy

16. Lenin was smuggled into Russia during the war from what country by what country?

    a.   From Britain by France
    b.   From Germany by France
    c.   From India by Britain
    d.   From Switzerland by Germany

17. Which of the following statements best applies to Lenin?

    a.   He was a central figure in the Provisional Government
    b.   In his "April Theses" he denounced revolutionary violence
    c.   His middle-class background made him want to establish a democratically-elected Russian Legislature
    d.   He promised that the Bolsheviks would redistribute all Russian lands to the peasants

18. The Second Battle of the Marne was

    a.   Germany's final effort to win the war
    b.   The decisive victory Germany had hoped to win
    c.   A disaster for the Allies
    d.   All of the above

19. At the end of the war, Woodrow Wilson wanted most of all to

    a.   Punish Germany
    b.   Assure self-determination for all peoples
    c.   Strengthen America's influence in Europe
    d.   Bring down the Soviet Union

20. At the Paris Peace Conference, Clemenceau of France wanted Germany to

    a.   Be demilitarized
    b.   Pay heavy reparations
    c.   Both of the above
    d.   Neither of the first two

Complete the Following Sentences:

1.   Among the ethnic minorities hoping in 1914 for nationhood were the _____ in Britain, the _____ in Russia, and the _____ in Austria-Hungary.

2.   Archduke Francis Ferdinand's assassin was a _____ who worked for a _____ terrorist organization called the _____ _____.

3.   A French counterattack under General _____ stopped the German army at the _____ River and led to a long period of _____ warfare.

4.   The great slaughters of World War I's Western Front occurred in the German offensive at _____, the British campaign on the _____, and the French attack in the _____.

5.   A British war humor magazine said there were two kinds of DUDS: one, a _____ that fails to explode; two an official who draws a big _____ and _____ for no reason.

6.   The United States was at last drawn into World War I in April, _____ by the German decision to use unrestricted _____ _____.

7.   When General _____ and his deputy _____ took control of the German government in 1916, they mobilized for _____ _____.

8.   David Lloyd George, who became the British _____ _____ in 1916, believed that the war would eliminate domestic _____ conflict.

9.   The 1917 March Revolution in Russia established a _____ Government, but it was overthrown within a year by the _____ led by _____.

10. American president Woodrow Wilson came to Paris with a plan for peace, his _____ _____, but he was met by resistance from leaders of _____ and _____ who wanted to punish Germany.

Place the Following in Chronological Order and Give Dates:

1.   Treaty of Brest-Litovsk signed   1.

2.   Armistice between Allies and Germany   2.

3.   Second Battle of the Marne   3.

4.   Paris Conference begins   4.

5.   Archduke Francis Ferdinand assassinated 5.

6.   Beginning of World War I   6.

7.   The United States enters the war   7.

Questions for Critical Thought:

1.   What were the conditions, factors, and events that led—both directly and indirectly—to the outbreak of World War I?

2.   Chart the development of the Great War in its two-year periods. Explain why it went on for so long and what finally hastened its end.

3.   What impact did a total war such as World War I have on life back home, in the countries involved? How were domestic, economic, and political moments affected by it?

4.   How did World War I lead to the revolution in Russia? How did it affect that final outcome of that internal struggle?

5.   Recount the story of the Russian Revolution, from the abdication of the Tsar, until the end of the ensuing civil war. How do these events help explain Russia today?

6.   How did the other national revolutions, in Austria and Germany, differ from the one in Russia? What accounts for the differences?

7.   Describe the Paris Peace Conference and the Treaty of Versailles. To what degree and in what ways were they and were they not successful?

Analysis of Primary Source Documents:

1. Describe how the emperors of Germany and Russia interpreted the events of July 1914 so differently. What bases for compromise were still open at that time, and why did they not prove useful?

2. Describe and explain the exhilaration people seemed to feel entering the Great War. What lessons were they about to learn?

3. Why would you know, had you not been told, that Remarque himself had known trench warfare? Explain why his account of it is so powerful.

4. Compare and contrast the songs sung about the Great War by Germans, British, and Americans. What national experiences and characteristics may be seen in the words?

5. What does Naomi Loughnan indicate she learned in her munitions factory about working-class men and women? What were various classes and genders learning from each other there?

6. What do his brief letters tell you about John Mott? What is the reason for and meaning of his constant understatement?

7. From John Reed's account, what do you think made Lenin the leader of the Russian Revolution? What does Reed mean by Lenin's "intellect"?

8. How did Woodrow Wilson and Georges Clemenceau differ in their assessments of the war? Why did Clemenceau consider Wilson naive and Wilson consider Clemenceau a vindictive bigot?

Map Exercise 15: Europe in 1914

Using various shades of pencil, color and label the following:

1. North Africa
2. Austria-Hungary
3. Belgium
4. Britain
5. France
6. Germany
7. Greece
8. Italy
9. Netherlands
10. Ottoman Empire
11. Russia
12. Serbia
13. Spain
14. Switzerland

Pinpoint and label the following:

1. Aisne River
2. Amiens
3. Antwerp
4. Argonne
5. Berlin
6. Brest-Litovsk
7. Brussels
8. Calais
9. Chateau Thierry
10. Cologne
11. Frankfurt
12. Gallipoli
13. LeHavre
14. Luxemburg

15. Marne River
16. Masurian Lakes
17. Mons
18. Moscow
19. Nancy
20. Oise River
21. Paris
22. St. Mihiel
23. Sedan
24. Seine River
25. Somme River
26. Tannenberg
27. Versailles
28. Vienna

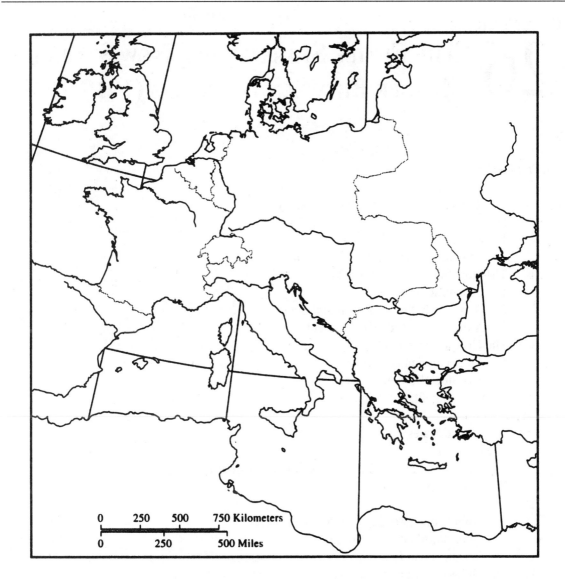

0   250   500   750 Kilometers

0   250   500 Miles

26 THE FUTILE SEARCH FOR A NEW STABILITY: EUROPE BETWEEN THE WARS (1919-1939)

Chapter Outline:

I.   An Uncertain Peace: The Search for Security
    A.   French Policy of Coercion, 1919-1924
        1.   Reparations and Occupation
        2.   Economic Crisis and Conciliation
    B.   The Hopeful Years, 1924-1929
        1.   Economic Stability
        2.   Germany in the League of Nations
        3.   A Plan for World Disarmament
    C.   The Great Depression
        1.   American Funds Withdrawn
        2.   The Stock Market Crash
        3.   Governmental Inaction

II. The Democratic States
    A.   Great Britain
        1.   Stanley Baldwin's Conservative Era of Prosperity
        2.   A Nation Government Coalition
    B.   France
        1.   From National Bloc to Cartel of the Left
        2.   Leon Blum's Popular Front
    C.   The Scandinavian Example of Social Democracy
    D.   The United States and Roosevelt's New Deal
        1.   American Government Involved
        2.   The Persistence of Unemployment

III. Retreat from Democracy: Authoritarian and Totalitarian States
    A.   Fascist Italy
        1.   The Anger of Post-war Italy

Chapter Summary:

Most intelligent observers knew by 1919 that the peace which ended World War I was flawed and insecure. The French, who felt vulnerable to another invasion and abandoned by their former allies, sought to weaken Germany and punish her for past offenses, leading to hostilities on both sides. There were a few hopeful years, during the late 1920s, with material prosperity seeming to return, but then the Great Depression of 1929 and following brought Europe back to the brink of ruin: economic, social, and political.

The democracies, Britain, France, the Scandinavian countries, and the United States, spent most of the 1930s trying to recover from the crash of 1929, while Eastern and Southern European nations turned even more to authoritarian and totalitarian governments. Following the lead of Fascist Italy, Germany surrendered to Nazi rule. Communism in Russia took a turn to the right under Stalin's iron fist. While Fascism and Communism espoused widely varied philosophies of economics and government, they showed striking similarities in their treatment of their people. Democracy seemed to be on the wane.

Popular culture reflected the deepening pessimism of the 1930s. While entertainment was more accessible than ever before, through rapid increases in the numbers of movie theaters and radios, while there was more time and opportunity for leisure activities than ever, people seemed driven to pleasure as if it might soon end, as a relief from the concerns of real life. Even film, radio, and leisure were used by the totalitarian regimes to increase their power. The arts, literature, and music reflected the pessimism and irrationality of the day; and physics continued to develop methods that might just as well destroy as save the world. Thunderclouds were gathering.

Identify:

1. Gustav Stresemann

2. Kellogg-Briand Pact

3. Cartel of the Left

4. Benito Mussolini

5. *Avanti*

6. Fascism

7. *Il Duce*

8. Weimar Republic

9.   Beer Hall *Putsch*

10. *Mein Kampf*

11. "Hitler Over Germany"

12. Gleichschaltung

13. The Third Reich

14. Aryanism

15. NEP

16. Joseph Pilsudski

17. Thomas Masaryk

18. Oswald Spengler

19. Igor Stravinsky

20. James Joyce

Match the Following Words with their Definitions:

1. Locarno

2. Stanley Baldwin

3. Leon Blum

4. March on Rome

5. Lateran Accords

6. *Lebensraum*

7. Franz von Papen

8. Oswald Spengler

9. Salvador Dali

10. Carl Jung

A. Fascist resolution of Italy's religious question

B. Served as prime minister for the Popular Front coalition

C. Nazi explanation for Eastern expansionism

D. Believed the West decadent and ready to fall

E. Pioneer in the Surrealist school of modern art

F. Disciple of Freud who studied the "collective unconscious"

G. Where Germany's western borders were guaranteed

H. Author of the arrangement that brought Hitler to power in Germany

I. Leader of British Conservatives during the prosperous 20s

J. Action that brought Mussolini to power in Italy

Choose the Correct Answer:

1. Efforts to maintain peace following World War I included:

    a. A three-power alliance of Britain, France, and Germany
    b. The development of a peace-keeping League of Nations army
    c. Only a weak alliance between France and the Little Entente
    d. Increasing intervention of the United States in Europe

2. The period 1924-1929 in Europe witnessed

    a. A growing optimism that liberal governments would provide peace and prosperity
    b. The Great Depression worsen and swallow Europe
    c. Continued occupation of all Germany by France and Britain
    d. Western nations cut off all ties with Russia

3.   A major cause of the Great Depression was

    a.   European unconcern for Asian affairs
    b.   The recall of American loans from European markets
    c.   High prices of agricultural products from eastern Europe
    d. . The Keynesian philosophy of free markets

4.   Economist John Maynard Keynes suggested that a way out of the Great Depression might be a

    a.   System of planned unemployment
    b.   Program of strict austerity to toughen the economy
    c.   Government program of public works
    d.   Series of government loans to business

5.   One overall effect of the Great Depression in Europe was

    a.   The fall of all Communist governments
    b.   High unemployment everywhere but in Britain
    c.   A strengthening of liberal democracies
    d.   The rise of fascist movements and governments

6.   The first Popular Front government of France

    a.   Solved the Depression by eliminating worker benefits
    b.   Was led by Socialist Leon Blum, who instituted a French "New Deal"
    c.   Was led by Fascist Jacques Boulanger, who reoccupied the Ruhr Valley
    d.   Collapsed in 1926, when the Cartel of the Left took power

7.   The assassination of Giacomo Matteotti by Fascists in 1924

    a.   Caused Mussolini to pull out of public life for five years
    b.   Won the Fascists unprecedented support in the 1924 elections
    c.   Forced Mussolini to make a push for full dictatorship
    d.   Led to the passage of the Acerbo Law

8. Which of the following statements best describes Mussolini's Italian Fascist state?

    a. Government control of the mass media allowed the state to successfully integrate the masses into its programs
    b. Fascist propaganda, laws, and practices attempted to force women out of factories and to stay at home
    c. Giuseppe Bottai's radical education policies enabled the state to create thousands of "new Fascist men"
    d. All religion, including Catholicism, was seen as the enemy of obedience to the state

9. Mussolini's Fascist dictatorship

    a. Lacked a secret police force
    b. Included highly popular, well attended youth meetings
    c. Was primarily aimed at aiding workers and peasants
    d. Never achieved the degree of totalitarianism found in Germany and Russia

10. The Lateran Accords of 1929

    a. Nationalized all church property
    b. Recognized Catholicism as the sole religion of Italy
    c. Coincided with the Catholic Church's official condemnation of Fascism
    d. Eliminated all government support for the Catholic Church

11. Adolf Lanz, a former monk, through his writings helped form Hitler's belief in

    a. A planned economy to benefit the workers
    b. Saying prayers three times a day, facing Jerusalem
    c. The superiority of the Aryan race
    d. A democratically run political party

12. On *Kristallnacht*, the German Nazis

    a. Burned Jewish synagogues
    b. Celebrated their first electoral majority victory
    c. Attacked Catholic churches
    d. Regrouped after their first electoral defeat

13. Heinrich Himmler was responsible for

    a. Forming Nazi professional organizations, such as doctors and teachers, to serve the state
    b. Carrying out SS operations of social and racial terror
    c. Chairing the German Labor Front
    d. Organizing the Hitler Youth organization

14. Stalin made his way to power in the Soviet Union as

    a. Secretary of the Communist Party, making appointments
    b. Commissioner of Labor, building the Moscow subway
    c. Defense Minister, successfully defeating the Poles
    d. Director of the Corps of Engineers, building dams

15. The Spanish Civil War ended with the victory of

    a. King Alfonso XIII and General Primo de Rivera
    b. An antifascist coalition, aided by Soviet troops
    c. The national front, aided by Italy and Germany
    d. General Francisco Franco, who established an authoritarian regime

16. *Dopolavoro* and *Kraft durch Freude* were programs designed by fascist governments to

    a. Increase the number of children each family produced
    b. Increased military awareness and preparedness
    c. Expand production in factories
    d. Provide civilian recreation but used to mold public opinion

17. Strength through Joy was

    a. Goebbels' effective Nazi propaganda film
    b. Fascist Italy's national recreation program
    c. An attempt to monitor and homogenize the leisure activities of German workers
    d. Failed miserably to draw Russian workers to join vacation package tours to the West

18. Arnold Schonberg was best known for his

    a. Socialist Realism paintings
    b. Atonal experimental music
    c. Revolutionary new directions in drama
    d. Theory of the Collective Unconscious

19. Nazi Art of Germany centered around

    a.   The use of abstract figures to reflect the New Order
    b.   Functionism as represented in the Bauhaus School
    c.   Realistic scenes that glorified the strong and heroic
    d.   A public display of sexuality

20. The physicist Werner Heisenberg was best known for

    a.   Proposing that uncertainty lay at the bottom of all physical laws
    b.   Being on the team that split the atom
    c.   Resurrecting the predictability of Newtonian physics
    d.   The final development of the Atomic Bomb

Complete the Following Sentences:

1. Although Woodrow Wilson originated the idea of a _____ of _____, his country's failure to join and refusal to honor defensive military alliances left _____ insecure and bitter, determined to keep _____ weak.

2. When Germany could not pay further _____, France occupied the _____ valley, and Germany then fueled _____ by printing more paper money.

3. John Maynard Keynes argued that unemployment stemmed from decline in _____ and that this could be remedied by _____ _____ projects, which could be financed by _____ _____.

4. The French Popular Front introduced new benefit programs for the _____ class, sometimes called the French _____ _____.

5. Benito Mussolini moved in his career from _____ _____ teacher to editor of _____ to founder of the _____ party.

6. In order to create his perfect Aryan state, the Nazis built death camps for _____ controlled the population with secret police directed by _____ _____, and trained children for Nazi service in the _____ _____.

7. By 1929 Stalin had secured power in Russia by eliminating all Old _____ from the Politburo, particularly _____ _____, who was eventually murdered at Stalin's orders in _____ in 1940.

8. Totalitarian states used recreation to mold their populations into willing servants of the leader, as is seen in the Fascist _____ and the Nazi _____ _____ _____.

9. The rebellious art movement called Dadaism tried to show the _____ of life by creating what it called _____, while the _____ Movement tried to visualize the unconscious.

10. In his masterpiece _____, the Irish exile James Joyce demonstrated the use of a literary "stream of _____" that would become a part of modern literature, using characters from his native city _____.

Place the Following in Chronological Order and Give Dates:

1.   *Kristallnacht* in Germany   1.

2.   Hitler dictatorship begins in Germany   2.

3.   Fascist dictatorship established in Italy   3.

4.   National Government coalition begins in Britain   4.

5.   Popular Front formed in France   5.

6.   New Deal begins in the United States   6.

7.   Stalin dictatorship begins in Russia   7.

Questions for Critical Thought:

1.   Explain why the years 1924-1929 were called "The Hopeful Years." What were the hopes, and how were they dashed?

2.   What caused the Great Depression, and how did it change history?

3.   How did the Western democracies react and respond differently to the Great Depression? Explain why the reactions and responses were so varied.

4. Describe and explain the European retreat from democracy and move toward totalitarianism in the time between the wars. Why did this happen where it happened, and what were the consequences?

5. Discuss the Nazi movement and its rise to power. What part did Adolf Hitler play? What kind of state and society did Nazism build?

6. What happened in the Soviet Union between the wars? How does the Stalinist era help explain contemporary events there?

7. What forms did art, music, philosophy, and literature take between the wars? How are these forms reflections of the age?

Analysis of Primary Source Documents:

1. Describe the results of unemployment during the Great Depression. How would a fascist politician have appealed for the votes of unemployed men?

2. Compare the Pilgrim Trust report on unemployment to the description of Depression life by George Orwell. What common images and problems do you find?

3. From reading the article supposedly penned by Mussolini, what principles of Italian fascism do you see that found their way into German Nazism? What was there about fascism that posed a threat to internal minorities and to world peace?

4. What did Hitler say made him hate Jews? How had he been prepared for his Viennese reaction? Why does he not mention earlier experiences and other influences?

5. What did Hitler think mass political meetings accomplished? How did he try in speeches to maximize the effects of these meetings?

6. Explain how the Soviet collective farm worked and why there was continual resistance to it by peasants.

7. What picture of Nazi leisure trips do you get from S.D.P. reports? How do these "opposition in exile" reports betray their own biases?

8. Describe how Hermann Hesse's young character wrestles with his unknown self. Why was this struggle so widely read by young Americans during the 1960's?

THE DEEPENING OF THE EUROPEAN CRISIS: WORLD WAR II

Chapter Outline:

I. Prelude to War, 1933-1939
    A. The Role of Hitler
        1. The Doctrine of *Lebensraum*
        2. Russia's Perceived Weaknesses
        3. Racial Supremacy and Empire
    B. The "Diplomatic Revolution," 1933-1936
        1. Hitler's "Peaceful" Goals
        2. Repudiation of the Versailles Treaty
        3. Occupation of the Rhineland
        4. Alliance with Mussolini's Italy
    C. The Path to War, 1937-1939
        1. Annexation of Austria
        2. Czechoslovakia and "Munich"
        3. The Invasion of Poland

II. The Course of World War II
    A. Early Victory and Stalemate (1939-1941)
        1. Blitzkrieg and the British at Dunkirk
        2. The Fall of France and the Vichy Government
        3. The Prime Ministership of Winston Churchill
        4. The Battle of Britain
        5. The German Invasion of Russia
        6. The War in Asia
            a. Japan in China
            b. Pearl Harbor and America's Entry into the War
    B. The Turning Point (1942-1943)
        1. Germany's Defeat at Stalingrad
        2. Japan's Defeat at Midway

C.   The Last Years of the War (1944-1945)
    1.   Allied Victories in North Africa and Italy
    2.   The Allied Invasion of France on D-Day
    3.   Russian Victories in the East
    4.   Germany's Surrender
    5.   Hiroshima and the Surrender of Japan

III. The Nazi New Order
  A.   The Nazi Empire
    1.   Conquest of "Inferior" Peoples
    2.   New Resources in the East
    3.   The Use of Foreign Labor
  B.   Resistance Movements
    1.   Tito in Yugoslavia
    2.   DeGaulle's Free French
    3.   The Communists
    4.   The Plot to Kill Hitler
  C.   The Holocaust
    1.   Aryan Supremacy
    2.   Emigration: The Madagascar Plan
    3.   The Final Solution
    4.   Concentration Camps: Experimentation and Death
    5.   Gypsies, Slavs, and Homosexuals

IV. The Home Front
  A.   The Mobilization of Peoples
    1.   A Planned Economy for Britain
    2.   Supercentralization in the Soviet Empire
    3.   Partial Mobilization of the American Economy
    4.   Late Total Mobilization in Germany
  B.   The Frontline Civilians: The Bombing of Cities
    1.   Attack Upon London
    2.   British Retaliation Against German Cities
    3.   The Bombing of Japan and the Atomic Attack Upon Hiroshima and Nagasaki

V.   The Aftermath of the War: The Emergence of the Cold War
  A.   Wartime Allied Conferences
    1.   Teheran and Percentages of Political Influence
    2.   Yalta and Roosevelt's Ideal of Self-Determination
    3.   Potsdam and Growing Mistrust
    4.   Churchill's "Iron Curtain" Speech

Chapter Summary:

World War II was the eruption of long simmering animosities and frustrations; and its outcome, both decisive and ambiguous, determined the course of European history for the next fifty years. It was also in a real sense the only truly world war in human history, and it helped set the global agenda for the rest of the Twentieth Century.

If we were to name one person as the key to the war, that person would be Germany's Adolf Hitler. Germany's bitterness over the outcome of the first war would indeed have been present without Hitler, as would Germany's industrial might and capacity to wage war, as would the vacuum of power in Central Europe; but Hitler and his Nazi Party gave voice and direction to these potentially dangerous factors. Implicitly understanding how reluctant the democracies were to fight another war, he moved to enlarge the frontiers of his Third Reich until his aggression was no longer tolerable and war began.

The first two years of the war, following the invasion of Poland in September, 1939, belonged to the Axis nations: Germany, Italy, and Japan. All the victories were theirs. Not until early in 1942, with America now allied to Britain and the Soviet Union, did the war turn. After Hitler's failure in Russia, after Italy's failure to resist Allied forces from North Africa, after the United States gained sea superiority against Japan, after the Allies successfully invaded France, the war wound down to its conclusion.

The Nazi Empire had done its bloody worst in all the lands it had held. Despite the effectiveness of resistance movements everywhere, Nazi forces dominated much of the continent for five years, bringing oppression and death to Jews, minorities, and all "inferior" peoples. Indiscriminate bombing of civilian areas by both sides led to a tragic number of innocent deaths. World War II was costly in every way.

Even before the German and Japanese surrender, the victors were having trouble agreeing on the post-war world; and at the various conferences held to determine borders and governments it was evident that a separation between East and West was inevitable. World War II was ending as tragically as World War I. The Cold War was beginning.

Identify:

1. *Lebensraum*

2. Neville Chamberlain

3. Kurt von Schuschnigg

4. Sudetenland

5. Danzig

6. *Blitzkrieg*

7. Henri Pétain

8. Vichy

9. *Luftwaffe*

10. Lend-lease

11. Grand Alliance

12. El Alamein

13. Midway

14. Charles de Gaulle

15. Holocaust

16. Zyklon B

17. Night Witches

18. Hiroshima

19. Cold War

20. Iron Curtain

Match the Following Words with their Definitions:

1. Munich

2. Dunkirk

3. Stalingrad

4. Midway

5. Madagascar

6. Auschwitz

7. Coventry

8. Dresden

9. Yalta

10. Potsdam

A. German camp designed to implement the Final Solution

B. Siege in which Germany's Sixth Army was lost

C. German city completely destroyed by British

D. Site of worst British defeat of the war

E. Site of conference that confirmed post-war mistrust among the Allies

F. Site of sea battle that made the U.S. superior to Japan in the Pacific

G. Site of conference that created the United Nations

H. Proposed as site for resettlement of European Jews

I. British city completely destroyed by German bombing

J. Site of conference that confirmed Hitler's belief that the democracies were weak

Choose the Correct Answer:

1. World War II was largely caused by

    a. Britain's aggressive behavior in Europe
    b. A power vacuum in Central Europe that only Germany could really fill
    c. Soviet expansionism and interference in Western European affairs
    d. Foolish posturing on the part of the League of Nations

2. When Hitler came to power, Germany was

    a. The most powerful state in Europe
    b. Limited by the Treaty of Versailles to an army of 100,000
    c. Threatened by Poland and Czechoslovakia
    d. Already massing troops in the Rhineland

3. The British policy of appeasement was based on

    a. The cowardly nature of the British upper class
    b. Admiration for the Germans and their culture
    c. Hatred and distrust of the French
    d. The conviction that it would maintain stability and peace

4. The Munich Conference was

    a. Applauded by Churchill as a "wise and noble experiment"
    b. Successful in keeping the Germans out of the Sudetenland
    c. Criticized by Churchill for setting a bad precedent
    d. A severe political setback for Hitler at home

5. Following the Allied evacuation at Dunkirk, France

    a. Soon surrendered and the Vichy government was established as a puppet to Germany
    b. Went on the offensive and stopped Germany in Normandy
    c. Called on Italy to help them fight the Germans
    d. Called on the Americans to move across from North Africa

6. The Grand Alliance of World War II made its first goal

    a. The defeat of Japan
    b. The defeat of Germany
    c. Liberation of African colonies taken by Germany
    d. Liberation of Asian colonies taken by Japan

7. The war in North Africa was best characterized by

    a. The overwhelming superiority of Italian troops
    b. Hitler's lack of commitment to take the Suez Canal
    c. Hitler's easy lines of supply that let the war drag on
    d. Heavy fighting due to the importance of its rubber supply

8. The turning point of the North African campaign came

    a. At El Alamein, where the British stopped Rommel in the summer of 1942
    b. When South African troops crossed the Sahara and overwhelmed Rommel
    c. When the free French revolted against the Vichy regime in Algeria
    d. When the Italians changed sides and joined the Allies in the fall of 1942

9.   After the attack on Pearl Harbor, the main priority of the United States was to

   a.   Defeat Japan as quickly as possible
   b.   Recover the Hawaiian Islands
   c.   Defeat Germany and then turn all of its resources against Japan
   d.   Remain neutral, while buying time to build back its industrial and military supplies

10.   Hitler's grand plan would have made the Slavic peoples

   a.   Independent of France
   b.   Slaves to the triumphant Germans
   c.   Soldiers in the army of the Third Reich
   d.   The richest farmers in the world

11.   Hitler's intentions for his conquests to the east included

   a.   Making the area a giant coal mine
   b.   Setting up a puppet Slavic state as a buffer against Russia
   c.   Massive colonization of the area by Germans
   d.   The creation of a wildlife preserve without human settlers

12.   The turning point in the war for eastern Europe was

   a.   The German fiasco at Stalingrad
   b.   The German victory at Leningrad
   c.   The Russian victory at Kiev
   d.   The Russian fiasco outside Moscow

13.   American naval superiority in the Pacific was

   a.   Never in question, even after Pearl Harbor
   b.   Precarious throughout and not achieved until the very end
   c.   Achieved beyond dispute after the Battle of Midway
   d.   Not a question because the Americans had no intentions of fighting a naval war

14.   The Allied advance in Italy was

   a.   Extremely slow due to staunch Italian resistance
   b.   Extremely rapid with all of Italy taken by November 1943
   c.   Greatly aided by Soviet troops invading from the north
   d.   Quite slow due to an effective German defense

15. The Nazi Empire was

    a.   Well organized into efficient states
    b.   Never much larger than Germany and Austria
    c.   Never well organized or efficiently governed
    d.   Composed of independent states that willingly cooperated with Hitler

16. The Nazi rule was most ruthless in

    a.   Eastern Europe where the Slavs were considered racial inferiors
    b.   France because of the age-old rivalry between the Germans and the French
    c.   Norway, Denmark, and the Netherlands because they were so geographically near the Fatherland
    d.   Italy because the Germans did not trust them

17. A major source of resistance to the Nazis came from

    a.   Germans who never really liked Hitler
    b.   Communists, especially after the invasion of Russia
    c.   The Vichy French who were the bravest of the Allies
    d.   The Austrians who believed they were the true Aryans

18. Nazi atrocities at Auschwitz

    a.   Were largely the exaggeration of war propagandists
    b.   Were willingly carried out by SS men who had few qualms about killing
    c.   Were limited to Jews, with other despised groups sent to work camps
    d.   Included cruel and painful "medical" experiments on inmates

19. Civilian bombing was carried out mainly to

    a.   Reduce the number of people available to be drafted
    b.   Exact revenge on the enemy
    c.   Break the will of the people to resist
    d.   Satisfy the appetite of bloody leader for high death counts

20. The official reason for dropping atomic bombs on Japan was

    a.   To punish Japan for the bombing of Pearl Harbor
    b.   The testing of new weapons for later battles
    c.   The shortage of explosive materials in the U.S. arsenal
    d.   To save the American lives an invasion of Japan would incur

Complete the Following Sentences:

1. In 1936 Hitler's army occupied the _____, and in 1938 he annexed _____, convinced that the democracies were _____.

2. At Munich, Chamberlain followed a policy of _____ toward Hitler, giving him courage to conquer _____.

3. After the Nazi invasion of _____ led to World War II, Hitler used "lightning war" or in German _____ to take Denmark, Norway, Netherlands, Belgium, and finally _____.

4. Germany occupied three-fifths of France but permitted Marshal _____ to establish a government in the rest, with a capital at _____.

5. World War II had started in Asia in 1937 when Japan invaded _____; and the United States placed trade sanctions against Japan for occupying _____; but war between Japan and the U.S. started with Japan's bombing of _____ _____.

6. In 1942 the Allies stopped Rommel in _____ _____; the German army failed to take the Russian city of _____; and the U.S. defeated Japan in the Battle of _____ _____.

7. After Hitler invaded Russia, _____ across Europe began leading movements of resistance to Nazism, but within Germany all resistance, such as the White _____ movement, were brutally crushed by the _____.

8. While early suggestions such as the _____ Plan would have sent European Jews into exile, the Final Solution as carried out by S.S. Security Service head _____ _____ was systematic _____.

9. The only World War II country to use women in combat, _____, trained female pilots, called _____.

10. Convinced that an invasion of Japan might cause a million _____ deaths, Harry Truman ordered an atomic bomb dropped first on _____ and then on _____.

Place the Following in Chronological Order and Give Dates:

1.   German surrender at Stalingrad   1.

2.   U.S. drops atomic bombs on Japan   2.

3.   Battle of Britain   3.

4.   German occupation of the Rhineland   4.

5.   Allied invasion of France   5.

6.   German invasion of Poland   6.

7.   Japanese attack Pearl Harbor   7.

Questions for Critical Thought:

1.   Describe the "diplomatic revolution" that Hitler began after 1933. Explain how this revolution led eventually to war.

2.   Trace the steps to war between 1935 and 1939. Who were the major figures in the drama, and what part did each one play?

3.   Tell the story of the first two years of World War II. If you had been reporting from the field in October 1942, what would you have predicted? Why?

4.   Explain why late 1942-1943 was the "turning point" of World War II. What people and events helped make it so?

5.   Describe the Nazi Empire: its organization, what it sought to accomplish, and its relative success. How does the Holocaust fit into the overall picture?

6.   Compare and contrast the way Britain, Russia, Germany and America mobilized their civilian populations for the war effort. What effects did each one's plan have on the outcome?

7.   Describe what it was like to live in a "front line" city during the war. To what extent did bombing affect the outcome of the war?

8.   Reviewing the Big Three wartime conferences, show the origins of the Cold War. Where exactly were crucial mistakes made—and by whom?

Analysis of Primary Source Documents:

1. What did Hitler mean by "sufficient living space" for Germany? Where did his vision lead him and his nation?

2. Compare and contrast the two interpretations—by Churchill and Chamberlain—of the Munich agreement. At that point in history, which sounded more plausible? Explain.

3. Using the German soldier's diary, recount how the German army in Russia lost heart. Why do you not find this man cursing Der Fuhrer?

4. Describe Hitler's vision of the new society he would establish in Eastern Europe. How was it to be achieved? What were its strengths and weaknesses?

5. Recount the systematic way people at German extermination camps were dispatched. What reasoning stood behind such a system?

6. How did aerial bombing change the nature and character of war? Describe its effects on people in cities under bombardment.

7. Show how the statements by Churchill and Stalin in March, 1946, illustrate the mutual mistrust that shaped the Cold War.

Map Exercise 16: World War II in Europe and North Africa

Using various shades of pencil, color and label the following:

1.   Allied powers Britain, Portugal, the U.S.S.R., the Middle East, and areas under allied control
2.   Axis powers—Germany and Italy
3.   Axis satellites and allies
4.   Conquests made by Axis 1939-1942
5.   Neutral nations

Pinpoint and label the following:

1.   Algiers
2.   Berlin
3.   Casablanca
4.   London
5.   Moscow
6.   Paris
7.   Rome
8.   Tunis
9.   Warsaw

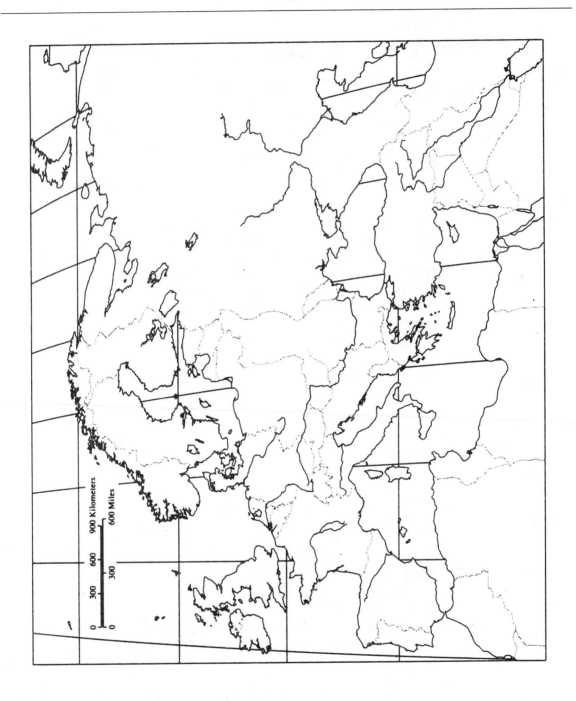

CHAPTER

28 COLD WAR AND A NEW EUROPE (1945-1970)

Chapter Outline:

I.   The Development of the Cold War
    A. Confrontation of the Superpowers
        1. Differing Historical Perspectives
        2. Disagreement Over Eastern Europe
        3. Greece, Turkey, and the Truman Doctrine
        4. Western Europe and the Marshall Plan
        5. The Kennan Theory of Containment
        6. The Troubled City of Berlin and the Airlift
        7. The Creation of NATO and the Warsaw Pact
        8. The Korean Conflict
    B. The Cuban Missile Crisis and Détente
        1. Fidel Castro's Cuba
        2. Kennedy, Khrushchev, and Crisis
        3. U.S. Involvement in Vietnam
        4. Steps Toward Better Relations Between the Superpowers

II. Recovery and Renewal in Europe
    A. The End of European Colonies
        1. Asia
        2. Africa
        3. The Third World
    B. The Soviet Union: From Stalin to Khrushchev
        1. Spectacular Economic Recovery
        2. Military Buildup and Technological Advance
        3. Khrushchev and Destabilization
        4. Eastern Europe: Behind the Iron Curtain
            a. Tito and Yugoslavia
            b. Stalinized States
            c. Khrushchev's Denunciation of Stalin and Revolt in Czechoslovakia

C. Western Europe's Revival of Democracy and the Economy
   1. France and Charles DeGaulle
      a. The Algerian Crisis and the Fall of the Fourth Republic
      b. DeGaulle and the Fifth Republic
   2. West Germany
      a. Konrad Adenauer and Rearmament
      b. Ludwig Erhard and Economic Recovery
      c. Denazification
   3. Great Britain and the Welfare State
      a. Clement Atlee and Economic Nationalization
      b. The Suez Crisis and Britain's Loss of Superpower Status
   4. Italy's Weak Coalition Governments
D. Western Europe's Move Toward Unity
   1. Experiments in Cooperation
   2. The Common Market

III. The United States and Canada: A New Era
   A. America in the 1950s
   B. Upheaval in the 1960s
   C. The Development of Canada

IV. The Emergence of a New Society
   A. The Structure of European Society
      1. Further Urbanization
      2. Rising Incomes and More Leisure Time
      3. The Welfare State
      4. Women in the Postwar Western World
      5. Feminism and the Search for Liberation
   B. The Permissive Society
      1. Sexual Freedom
      2. Divorce
      3. Drugs
   C. Education and Student Revolt

Chapter Summary:

No sooner had the Allies defeated the Central Powers than they began bickering among themselves. The democracies helped to see a Europe of representative governments and free markets, while the Soviets wanted to create a buffer against further threats from the West. In the end, what Winston Churchill called an Iron Curtain descended across the continent, separating East from West. The Cold War began.

Distrust grew as each side came to see the other as a menace to safety in the world. The Cold War, made all the more dangerous by the presence on both sides of nuclear weapons, continued through much of the rest of the Twentieth Century, dominating foreign policy in all European countries. Only after the Cuban Missile Crisis of 1963, when world survival seemed questionable, did the two sides begin the first tentative steps toward détente.

Meanwhile the faces of Europe and indeed the world was changed in the years just after the war. While the Soviet Union created Stalinist satellites out of the formerly independent nations surrounding it, the Western democracies experimented with social reform that led in many countries to the welfare state. Britain led the way by efforts, under the Labour government that came to power in the first postwar election, to provide social security for all its citizens: insurance, healthcare, pensions. Western Europe grouped together militarily in the North Atlantic Treaty Organization and economically in the organization of the Common Market.

Society changed during the period from 1945 to 1970. Citizen protests of the status quo occurred on both sides of the Iron Curtain. In Hungary and in Czechoslovakia of the Soviet bloc, in France and the United States of the West, people protesting materialism and injustice made their voices heard in demonstrations Everywhere in the West there was more freedom, yet there was also a feeling that society had lost its way. People everywhere seemed to be looking for a new solution to an aging set of problems.

Identify:

1. Harry Truman

2. George Kennan

3. Berlin Airlift

4. NATO

5. Warsaw Pact

6. Ho Chi Minh

7. Ngo Dinh Diem

8. Decolonization

9. Mao Zedong

10. Nikita Khrushchev

11. Alexander Dubcek

12. Charles De Gaulle

13. Fifth Republic

14. Konrad Adenauer

15. Clement Atlee

16. Christian Democrats

17. Gamal Abdel Nasser

18. EEC

19. Welfare State

20. Herbert Marcuse

Match the Following Words with their Definitions:

1. Truman Doctrine

2. Marshall Plan

3. CENTO

4. SEATO

5. Sputnik

6. Alexander Solzhenitsyn

7. Josip Broz

8. Alexander Dubcek

9. Charles de Gaulle

10. Herbert Marcuse

A. Organization formed to save Asian countries from Chinese Communism

B. Permission to publish his novel demonstrated some liberalization in Russia

C. The first artificial earth satellite

D. Policy designed to prevent Communist aggression in Greece and Turkey

E. Leader of resistance to Nazis who later ruled Yugoslavia

F. Founder of the Fifth French Republic

G. Organization formed to save the Middle East from Russian aggression

H. Critic of capitalism who hoped for a student revolution

I. Program to restore Western Europe's economy

J. Czechoslovakian leader removed by Soviet show of force

Choose the Correct Answer:

1. The Truman Doctrine, which promised aid to countries resisting Communist domination, came in response to threats to

    a. Greece and Turkey
    b. Austria and Italy
    c. Lebanon and Israel
    d. Egypt and Iran

2.   The American plan to aid Europe's economic recovery was named for

    a.   Secretary of State Dean Acheson
    b.   Secretary of State George Marshall
    c.   President Harry Truman
    d.   President Dwight D. Eisenhower

3.   The Cold War struggle over Germany resulted in

    a.   The creation of an independent united Germany under Walter Ulbricht
    b.   An East German economic miracle brought about with Soviet technological advances
    c.   A successful blockade of West Berlin by Soviet forces
    d.   The creation of two separate German states

4.   American General Douglas MacArthur was leader during the Korean War of

    a.   An army made up almost entirely of South Korean peasant volunteers
    b.   Forces authorized and manned by the United Nations
    c.   The American Eighth Army
    d.   Forces sent to aid South Korea from China

5.   One overall effect of the Korean War was

    a.   The domination of Southeast Asia by the Soviet Union
    b.   An end to American and Soviet involvement in Asian affairs
    c.   The reinforcement of American determination to contain Soviet power in the world
    d.   An end to all Communist efforts to gain a foothold on the Asian continent

6.   The United States played a dominant role in all of the following alliances *except*

    a.   NATO
    b.   COMECON
    c.   CENTO
    d.   SEATO

7.   In 1963 President Kennedy responded to proof that there were nuclear weapons in Cuba with

    a.   An order to keep it secret so as not to disturb the American public
    b.   An invasion order that failed at the Bay of Pigs
    c.   A blockade of the island which required Soviet ships to turn back
    d.   An air attack that knocked out the missiles

8.   The Cuban Missile Crisis resulted in

    a.   Improved communications between the U.S. and the U.S.S.R.
    b.   The installation of more Soviet missiles in Cuba
    c.   An overthrow of the Castro regime sponsored by the United States
    d.   President Kennedy agreeing to all of Premier Khrushchev's demands

9.   Post-World War II life in the U.S.S.R. under Stalin saw

    a.   Continued low standards of living for the working classes
    b.   An emphasis on the production of luxury consumer goods
    c.   Relaxation of restrictions on artists and writers
    d.   The adaptation of Communist programs to new Western European ways

10.   The domestic policies of Nikita Khrushchev in the 1950s and early 1960s

    a.   Were basically a continuation of Stalin's policies
    b.   Were bolstered by his successes in foreign policy
    c.   Tried but failed to benefit the Soviet economy and industry
    d.   Focused on repressing intellectuals and artists

11.   The 1956 independence movement in Hungary resulted in

    a.   The end of Communist rule there
    b.   An end to American control of the economy
    c.   Armed Soviet intervention and the reassertion of strong Communist leadership
    d.   A revival of the Catholic faith among the Hungarian people

12.   The 1968 Czechoslovakian "Prague Spring"

    a.   Was triggered by the reforms of Alexander Dubcek
    b.   Led to the presidency in 1970 of Vaclav Havel
    c.   Saw Czechoslovakia withdraw from the Soviet bloc
    d.   Brought about the resignation of Gustav Husak

13.   As President of France, Charles de Gaulle's policy toward the Cold War was to

    a.   Align France with the Warsaw Pact nations
    b.   Remain independent of the superpowers
    c.   Follow the American lead throughout
    d.   Make France the leading member of NATO

14. The founding hero and first chancellor of the West German Federal Republic was

    a.   Helmut Kohl
    b.   Helmut Schmidt
    c.   Willy Brandt
    d.   Konrad Adenauer

15. Which of the following statements on postwar Britain is *false*?

    a.   National Insurance and National health acts helped make Britain a welfare state
    b.   The Conservative Party in the 1950s revoked nearly all of the socialist legislation of the
          Labour Party of the 1940s
    c.   Neither Labour nor the Conservatives could solve problems of labor, the economy, or
          Northern Ireland
    d.   Churchill served a second term before retiring

16. The Suez Crisis of 1956 ended the superpower pretenses of

    a.   Britain
    b.   France
    c.   The United States
    d.   The U.S.S.R.

17. Post-war Italian politics were characterized by

    a.   The dominance of the Communist Party
    b.   The demise of the Christian Democrats
    c.   Chronic instability among parliamentary coalitions
    d.   Constant interference by the Pope

18. The free trade union known as the Common Market included all of the following *except*

    a.   France
    b.   Spain
    c.   The United States
    d.   Italy

19. Herbert Marcuse expected a revolution against material values to be led by

   a. Stalinists dictators
   b. Unindoctrinated students
   c. American industrialists
   d. The Christian Socialist Parties

20. The outbreak of student revolts in the late 1960s was inspired by

   a. The war in Vietnam
   b. Overcrowded classrooms and lack of professional attention
   c. Discontent with materialism
   d. All of the above

Complete the Following Sentences:

1. U.S. President Truman was so alarmed in 1947 by _____ inability to defend the eastern Mediterranean that he offered American aid to protect _____ and _____ against Soviet expansion.

2. U.S. diplomat George Kennan, an expert in _____ affairs, influenced American policy for decades with his article in _____ _____ calling for _____ of Communism.

3. President Kennedy's response to discovering Soviet _____ in Cuba in 1962 was to _____ the island, then agree not to _____ it.

4. Post-war decolonization saw the United States leave the _____, Britain leave _____, and France leave _____.

5. For convenience after 1950 the industrialized nations came to be called the _____ _____, the Soviet sphere the _____ _____, and the poorer regions the _____ _____.

6. Khrushchev's criticism of _____ _____ encouraged such a spirit of rebellion in the Soviet _____ that he had to crush a 1956 uprising in _____ and one in 1968 in _____.

7. To make the case that France was in the 1950s still a great power, Charles de Gaulle withdrew from _____, built _____ weapons, and increased the production and export of _____ and _____.

8. In Germany, Ludwig Erhard's work as Minister of Finance helped bring about the post-war
    _____ _____, and he was rewarded by being chosen to succeed
    _____ _____ as chancellor.

9. The British welfare system, which inspired other European nations, nationalized the
    _____ of England, enacted a National _____ Act, and established a
    National _____ Service.

10. Across Europe various countries followed the Swedish "sexual revolution" of the 1960s by
    decriminalizing _____, providing more sex _____, and introducing a pill
    for _____.

Place the Following in Chronological Order and Give Dates:

1. Cuban missile crisis   1.

2. Formation of the Warsaw Pact   2.

3. Erection of the Berlin Wall   3.

4. Formation of NATO   4.

5. The Prague Spring   5.

6. Truman Doctrine outlined   6.

7. De Gaulle assumes power in France   7.

Questions for Critical Thought:

1. What were the causes of the Cold War? What issues continued through the 1950s and 1960s to
    divide East and West? Did world leaders make things better or worse?

2. Trace the American response to Communism from the Truman Doctrine through the Cuban
    Missile Crisis. What part did the theories of George Kennan play in the formulation of
    American policy?

3. How did "decolonization" affect both the First World and the Third World? What kind of
    world would we have today had "decolonization" been slower and more peaceful?

4. Trace the history of the Soviet Bloc from 1945 to 1970. To what degree did its rivalry with the West create its policies and directions? How did it in turn affect those in the West?

5. Explain Charles de Gaulle's foreign policy. How and why was it so different from that of most Western nations?

6. What areas of the citizen's life were affected by the experiments in the welfare state adopted by Western democracies after World War II? What are the benefits and problems of the welfare state?

7. Discuss the causes and effects of the "permissive" society of post-war Europe. In what ways are we still living under its influence?

Analysis of Primary Source Documents:

1. Explain the Truman Doctrine. What threat provoked it, what was its intent, and where did it lead? What similar threats later appeared, and how did subsequent presidents respond to them?

2. Compare Khrushchev's account of the Cuban Missile Crisis with what you know of the American version of this event. Who was really the aggressor, and who really won?

3. How does Franz Fanon's murder case demonstrate the brutalization of youth by social unrest? Name places in today's world where the same thing could happen.

4. What made Khrushchev denounce Stalin, the man he had served? What did his candor do for Communist Party credibility?

5. How does the 1956 uprising against Soviet rule in Hungary look today, when Hungary seems free of foreign domination? What now seems to be its significance? Will today's view continue?

6. Explain what Simone de Beauvoir meant by "the other." Why do men perpetuate this image, and why do women tolerate it?

7. If Bob Dylan's song is an anthem for the protest movement of the 1960s, whom did the protestors want to hear their protest and why?

8. Compare and contrast the two student proclamations of 1968. How do they reveal both the awareness and the naiveté of the student protest movements of the time?

THE CONTEMPORARY WESTERN WORLD (SINCE 1970)

Chapter Outline:

III. New Directions and New Problems in Western Society
   A.   The Women's Movement
   B.   Terrorism
       1.   Blows Against Capitalism
       2.   The Desire for Political Separatism
       3.   Anti-terrorist Plans
   C.   Guest Workers and Immigrants
       1.   Ethnic Conflict
       2.   Attacks on Foreigners
   D.   The Green Movement
       1.   Concern for the Environment
       2.   Political Action

IV. The World of Western Culture
   A.   Recent Trends in Art, Music, and Literature
       1.   Jackson Pollock's Abstract Impressionism
       2.   Andy Warhol's Pop Art
       3.   Olivier Messiaen's Serialism
       4.   Samuel Becket's Theater of the Absurd
   B.   The Philosophical Dilemma: Existentialism
       1.   Jean-Paul Sartre
       2.   Albert Camus
   C.   Revival of Religion
   D.   Science and Technology
       1.   The Computer
       2.   Military Technology
       3.   The Space Race
       4.   The "Small is Beautiful" Movement
   E.   Explosion of Popular Culture
       1.   Americanization of the World
       2.   New European Film Makers
       3.   Television
       4.   The Golden Age of Rock Music
       5.   Mass Sports

V. Toward a Global Civilization?
   A.   Global Problems
   B.   Nongovernmental Organizations
   C.   International Cooperation

Chapter Summary:

The Western world has seen amazing changes during the past twenty years. The most remarkable of these has been the disintegration of the Soviet Union and the release of its dependent countries. As late as 1980 the Cold War was still being waged by both sides in the ideological struggle between Capitalism and Communism; but by 1990 the entire picture had changed.

Beginning with Mikhail Gorbachev's attempt to reform the Soviet economy, pressure for change gathered such strength that the Soviet Union was dissolved and all the countries that were once a part of its sphere of influence were freed to go their own ways. Germany was reunited, while Yugoslavia crumbled into warring factions. Old enemies became friends in an effort to cope with threats of chaos from many sides, while ethnic groups once forcibly combined under single national banners began pulling apart to create autonomous states. The world about to enter the Twenty-first Century looked quite different from the one formed just after World War II.

While the "new world order" was just becoming evident, the challenges and problems facing it were already clear. Terrorism sponsored by dissident groups, tensions caused by the presence of alien residents in many countries, and threats to humankind from environmental abuses are the issues to occupy attention and energies for the foreseeable future. New trends in the arts, literature, the sciences, philosophy and religion reflect both the tensions of the Cold War now past and the uncertainties that come with its demise.

At present it is clear to all thoughtful people, that in order to cope with the dangers and realize the opportunities in our future we must begin to think globally. The nation-state, for so long the decisive institution in Western man's life, must take second place to the state of humankind if we are all to live full lives in peace with ourselves and the environment. The heroes of the future may be the men and women who show the way to think and live in this fashion.

Identify:

1. "Evil empire"

2. "Star Wars"

3. Mikhail Gorbachev

4. *Perestroika*

5. *Glasnost*

6. Chernobyl

7. Boris Yeltsin

8. Solidarity

9. Vaclav Havel

10. Slobodan Miloševi?

11. Helmut Kohl

12. "Iron Lady"

13. Francois Mitterand

14. Pierre Trudeau

15. Pop Art

16. Serialism

17. Samuel Beckett

18. Albert Camus

19. Karl Rahner

20. E.F. Schumacher

Match the Following Words with their Definitions:

1.	*Détente*	A.	Leader of the Solidarity movement in Poland
2.	Kuwait	B.	Leader in the Pop Art movement
3.	*Perestroika*	C.	Playwright in the Theater of the Absurd
4.	Lech Walesa	D.	Site of first post-Cold War military cooperation between the U.S. and the U.S.S.R.
5.	Vaclav Havel		
6.	Andy Warhol	E.	Film maker who raised his art to the level of the novel
7.	Olivier Messiaen	F.	Leading exponent of existentialist philosophy
8.	Samuel Beckett	G.	Gorbachev's plan for restructuring the Soviet system
9.	Jean-Paul Sartre		
10.	Ingmar Bergman	H.	First serialist composer
		I.	Playwright who became President of Czechoslovakia
		J.	An easing of Cold War tensions between East and West

Choose the Correct Answer:

1. Mikhail Gorbachev's plan of *perestroika* at first aimed at

   a. Market economy with complete free enterprise and homestead lands
   b. Market economy with some free enterprise and some private property
   c. Modified Marxism with the state controlling all businesses
   d. Return to pure marxism, which he believed had been too quickly abandoned

2. Gorbachev was surprised when his *glasnost* was used to advantage by

   a. Military officers to gain more power
   b. Religious leaders to restore their old privileges
   c. Ethic and national groups to press for more autonomy
   d. The old Communist guard to regain powers lost to democracy

3. Lech Walesa's Solidarity movement had the support of all the following *except*

    a. The Communist Party
    b. The Catholic Church
    c. Polish intellectuals
    d. Polish workers

4. In Romania the move to overthrow the Communist regime in 1989 ended with Chairman Ceausescu being

    a. Exiled to Russia
    b. Imprisoned for life
    c. Demoted to farm workers
    d. Tried and executed

5. With German reunification in 1990, the section that was formerly East Germany

    a. Became known as Middle Germany
    b. Was the richest part of the new nation
    c. Ceased to exist as a separate entity
    d. Kept its own legislature and currency

6. After Tito's death in 1980, Yugoslavia was plunged into civil war by Serbians calling for

    a. A restoration of the Catholic Faith in Bosnia
    b. New borders to accommodate Serb minorities
    c. Repayment of loans made by the World Bank
    d. Separate membership in NATO

7. The European Community remains today

    a. Too weak to affect world affairs
    b. Limited to former NATO Allies
    c. An organization dominated by Britain
    d. Purely an economic not a political union

8. Margaret Thatcher's popularity rose when she successfully prevented

    a. Argentina from taking the Falklands
    b. Mexico from taking Jamaica
    c. China from taking Hong Kong
    d. India from taking Burma

9. Feminists after 1960 were most successful in

    a. Gaining women positions on formerly men-only sporting teams
    b. Imitating men's styles in clothing
    c. Legalizing contraception and abortion
    d. Gaining "equal pay for equal work" for women

10. Name the group below that was not a terrorist organization of the 1970s and 1980s.

    a. German's Red Army Faction
    b. Scotland's Celtic Guard
    c. Italy's Red Brigades
    d. Britain's I.R.A.

11. Identify the *false* connection below.

    a. Andy Warhol—Pop Art
    b. Samuel Beckett—Theater of the Absurd
    c. Jackson Pollock—Abstract Expressionism
    d. Vaclav Havel—Serialist Music

12. After World War II, the world's art center moved

    a. From Europe to America
    b. From America to Europe
    c. From America to Japan
    d. From Europe to Japan

13. Jackson Pollock's art

    a. Represented a return to classical themes
    b. Assaulted viewers with emotion and movement
    c. Was too individualistic to have any influence on other artists
    d. Led to laws banning pornography

14. Like many other modern American composers, Philip Glass moved easily

    a. In political circles
    b. From town to town to find sponsors
    c. From classical to popular forms
    d. Across national boundaries to avoid paying taxes

15. "Theater of the Absurd" literature

    a. Is represented by Beckett's *Waiting for Godot*
    b. Reflects postwar disillusionment with religious and political ideologies
    c. Questions the ability of language to express reality
    d. All of the above

16. The philosophy of existentialism

    a. Dominated universities in Britain and the United States
    b. Was best expressed in the writings of Sartre and Camus
    c. Concentrated on logic and epistemology
    d. Prospered in the optimistic postwar world

17. Existentialism stressed

    a. The need for people to create their own values
    b. A return to the God of traditional religion
    c. The human capacity to discover the one true purpose of the world
    d. A withdrawal from the active life

18. The world of science after World War II witnessed all of the following *except*

    a. Most scientific funding going for military projects
    b. The dominance of government sponsorship in scientific research
    c. A return to Newtonian physics
    d. The merging of theoretical science with technology

19. Name the one below who was *not* an art film maker of the post-war period.

    a. Sweden's Ingmar Bergman
    b. France's Francois Truffaut
    c. Japan's Keiko Oh
    d. Italy's Federico Fellini

20. The sport that has become the number one expression of national identity and the most watched event on television throughout the world are

    a. Hockey and the Stanley Cup
    b. Soccer and the World Cup
    c. Football and the Super Bowl
    d. Gymnastics and the Olympics

Complete the Following Sentences:

1. Because he considered the Soviet Union an _____ _____, U.S. President Ronald Reagan proposed a Strategic Defense Initiative, nicknamed _____ _____.

2. The new friendship between the U.S. and Russia was tested in 1990 when Iraq invaded _____, precipitating the _____ War.

3. Poland's move from Communist rule to a free market economy was led by _____, a _____ movement directed by its president _____ _____.

4. In the former Yugoslavia, the Serbian move to rid Bosnia of Muslims, called _____ cleansing, revived memories of _____ atrocities during World War II; yet NATO forces did not strongly retaliate until _____ Bosnians had been killed.

5. At first greeted with euphoria, German reunification later brought high _____ and _____, and physical attacks on Germany's _____ population.

6. Margaret Thatcher's government in Britain broke the power of the _____ _____ and attacked _____ with austerity measures, but her popularity soared with victory in the _____ War.

7. Terrorism reached its peak in Italy when in 1978 former premier _____ _____ was kidnapped and killed by the _____ _____.

8. The 1986 disaster at _____ in the Soviet Union made the world more aware of the nuclear threat, and 1987 was proclaimed by Greens as the Year of the _____.

9. "Theater of the Absurd" is best represented by Irishman _____ _____ and his play _____ _____ _____.

10. Existentialism holds that while the _____ of God is tragic, it liberates man from any preordained _____ and makes him depend on _____.

Place the Following in Chronological Order and Give Dates:

1.   Helmut Kohl chosen Chancellor of West Germany   1.

2.   Dissolution of the U.S.S.R.   2.

3.   Francois Mitterand elected President of France   3.

4.   Reunification of Germany   4.

5.   Margaret Thatcher becomes British Prime Minister   5.

6.   Solidarity Movement emerges in Poland   6.

7.   Mikhail Gorbachev comes to power in the U.S.S.R.   7.

Questions for Critical Thought:

1.   What was Mikhail Gorbachev's part in the final act of the Cold War? How would events have been different without him? How will he be judged by future historians?

2.   What directions did the Eastern European nations take once Soviet control ended? Why did they react as they did? Will they change directions again? How and why?

3.   What were the major successes and failures of the Western European democracies after 1970? Was there enough unity among these countries as they sought to create an economic community to succeed?

4.   How did the feminist movement after World War II differ from its pre-war counterparts? Does it now seem at last to have found its true focus?

5.   Explain how modern movements in the arts and philosophy reflect both the uncertainty and the courage to experiment of the recent decades.

6.   How does contemporary religion, said to be in a period of revival, compare and contrast with its counterpart before World War II?

7.   Describe the new globalism. How and why did it develop? How does it relate to the technological and social concerns of our age? What might it achieve?

Analysis of Primary Source Documents:

1. What does Mikhail Gorbachev say made him decide a "restructuring" was necessary? In what sense is it needed everywhere as it is in the Soviet Union?

2. Describe what Vaclav Havel calls the "contaminated moral environment." Who is to blame, and what is the solution? Is this analysis too simple? Why or why not?

3. Show how the two news reports from the former Yugoslavia demonstrate the brutalizing effects of continuing war. Can you determine from these reports who is to blame for the war crimes?

4. What characteristics of a future British prime minister are evident in Thatcher's early entry into politics? Are her actions those of a feminist or not?

5. Given the violence aimed at foreigners living in Germany, to what extent does it appear the racism that produced Nazism is still alive and well there? What would you suggest the government do to solve the problem?

6. If Jean-Paul Sartre's definition is correct, what is the essence of the existentialist philosophy? What does the phrase "man is condemned to be free" mean?

7. What is Pope John Paul II's way of achieving world peace? To what degree could his philosophy be accepted by one who does not necessarily share his Catholic faith?

8. How does E.F. Schumacher say modern people are using their capital as if it were income? What is his solution? Will it work?

Map Exercise 17: The New Europe

On Map A label each nation and use different shades of pencil to color each one's affiliations in the Cold War:

1.   NATO bloc
2.   Warsaw Pact bloc
3.   Neutral nations
4.   Independent nations

On Map B label each nation and use different shades of pencil to color each one's identity:

1.   Members of the European Economic Community
2.   Former members of the U.S.S.R. now independent
3.   Eastern European nations, once in the Soviet bloc now independent

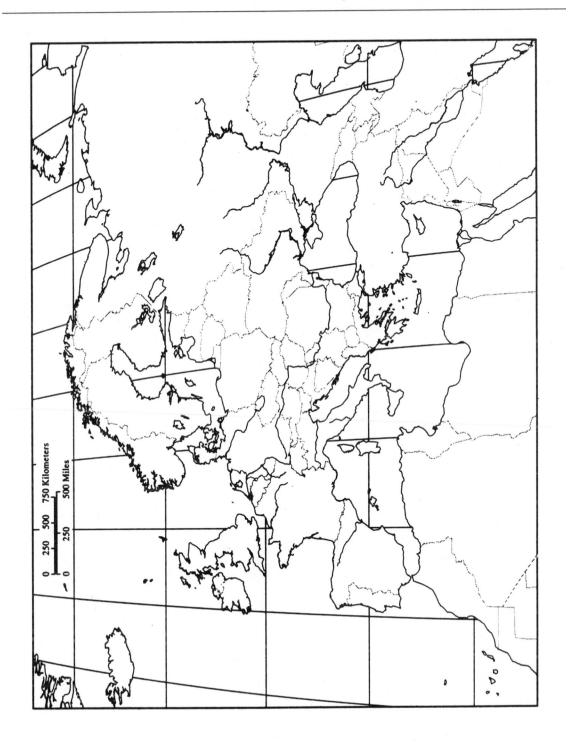

ANSWER KEY

CHAPTER 14

Matching

1. E
2. C
3. I
4. A
5. G
6. H
7. F
8. B
9. J
10. D

Multiple Choice

1. d
2. b
3. b
4. c
5. c
6. d
7. a
8. a
9. d
10. a
11. d
12. a
13. a
14. c
15. c
16. d
17. a
18. b
19. d
20. a

Completion

1. Navigator, Vasco da Gama, d'Albuquerque
2. Hernando Cortes, Francesco Pizarro, de Las Casas
3. Huguenots, Saint Bartholomew's, Guise
4. Supremacy, Elizabeth, Mary
5. Armada, Catholic, Scotland, Ireland
6. Religious, Bohemia, Westphalia
7. El Greco, mannerism, Toledo
8. Theresa, mystical, ecstacy
9. Religious, magistrate, disclose himself
10. Elizabeth, Lord Chamberlain's, Globe, Blackfriars

Chronology

1. Battle of Lepanto: 1571
2. Saint Bartholomew's Day Massacre: 1572
3. *Essays* published: 1580
4. Defeat of the Spanish Armada: 1588
5. Edict of Nantes: 1598
6. Death of Elizabeth: 1603
7. Peace of Westphalia: 1648

CHAPTER 15

Matching

1. J
2. H
3. G
4. C
5. B
6. E
7. A
8. D
9. I
10. F

Multiple Choice

1. d
2. b
3. d
4. c
5. a
6. b
7. c
8. a
9. b
10. a
11. d
12. c
13. a
14. a
15. b
16. a
17. c
18. c
19. b
20. d

Completion

1. Nantes, Fontainebleau
2. Finance, mercantilism, export, import
3. Grandson, Spanish Succession
4. Frederick William, army, Commissariat
5. Inquisition, Index, Jesuits
6. German suburb, Western, backward
7. Catholic, Orange, Mary
8. Constitutional, law, rights
9. Commerce, Rembrandt
10. *Misanthrope*, clergy

Chronology

1. Michael Romanov begins reign: 1613
2. *Leviathan* published: 1651
3. Turkish siege of Vienna: 1683
4. Edict of Fontainebleau: 1685
5. England's Glorious Revolution: 1688
6. Peter Romanov's trip to the West: 1697-98
7. War of Spanish Succession: 1702-1713

CHAPTER 16

Matching

1. H
2. D
3. A
4. J
5. G
6. B
7. D
8. I
9. E
10. F

Multiple Choice

1. d
2. a
3. b
4. d
5. d
6. a
7. a
8. b
9. a
10. c
11. c
12. c
13. d
14. a
15. b
16. d
17. b
18. c
19. b
20. d

Completion

1. Aristotle, Galen
2. Geometrizes, mathematical, Hermetic
3. Geocentric, Heliocentric, complicated
4. Mountains, moons, sun
5. Simplicio, Sagredo, Salviati
6. Calculus, light, gravity
7. Liver, veins, arteries
8. Mind, material world, Dualism
9. Synagogue, pantheist, God
10. Charles II, Louis XIV, practical

Chronology

1. Copernicus' *Revolutions*: 1543
2. Galileo's *Messenger*: 1610
3. Bacon's *Instauration*: 1620
4. Harvey's *Motion*: 1628
5. Descartes' *Method*: 1637
6. Pascal's *Pensées*: 1669
7. Newton's *Principia*: 1687

CHAPTER 17

Matching

1. E
2. D
3. I
4. G
5. A
6. J
7. B
8. C
9. F
10. H

Multiple Choice

1. a
2. b
3. a
4. d
5. a
6. c
7. d
8. b
9. b
10. c
11. d
12. c
13. a
14. c
15. b
16. c
17. c
18. c
19. d
20. b

Completion

1. *Historical and Critical Dictionary*, dogmatism
2. Catholic Church, monarchy, checks, balances
3. Deism, Jean Calas
4. *Encyclopedia*, independence, revolt, price
5. Mercantilism, agriculture
6. *Social Contract*, *Emile*, private property
7. Aristocratic, Vierzehnheiligen
8. *Messiah*, *Don Giovanni*
9. Louis XIV, Roman Empire
10. Education, Portugal, Spain, France

Chronology

1. Montesquieu's *Persian Letters*: 1721
2. Voltaire's *Philosophic Letters*: 1733
3. Diderot's *Encyclopedia* begun: 1751
4. Rousseau's *Social Contract*: 1762
5. Smith's *Wealth of Nations*: 1776
6. Gibbon's *Decline* completed: 1788
7. Condorcet's *Progress*: 1794

CHAPTER 18

Matching

1. D
2. I
3. J
4. G
5. A
6. B
7. H
8. E
9. C
10. F

Multiple Choice

1. d
2. d
3. b
4. b
5. d
6. a
7. d
8. c
9. a
10. c
11. d
12. b
13. c
14. c
15. c
16. b
17. b
18. a
19. b
20. c

Completion

1. Pocket, landed
2. George III, French, Napoleon
3. Voltaire, speech, press, toleration
4. Maria Theresa, Philosophy
5. Emelyan Pugachev, executed, agrarian reform
6. 30, 50, Two
7. India, North America, empire
8. Wet nurses, clothes, toys
9. Cotton, coffee, sugar, slave
10. Sophisticated, art, women

Chronology

1. Hanoverian succession: 1714
2. Frederick the Great begins reign: 1740
3. Seven Years' War: 1756-63
4. Joseph II joins Maria Theresa: 1765
5. First Polish partition: 1772
6. Regicide of Louis XVI: 1792
7. Retirement of Pitt the Younger: 1801

CHAPTER 19

Matching

1. D
2. J
3. A
4. G
5. B
6. H
7. C
8. F
9. I
10. E

Multiple Choice

1. a
2. c
3. a
4. d
5. b
6. c
7. b
8. b
9. d
10. c
11. d
12. b
13. b
14. d
15. c
16. d
17. a
18. c
19. a
20. b

Completion

1. Stamp Act, tea
2. Thomas Paine, Second, 1776
3. Taxes, Versailles, Revolution
4. People, state, Civil Constitution
5. Girondin, Mountain, Mountain
6. Saint, Notre Dame, marry
7. Brumaire, Germinal, Fructidor
8. Virtue, guillotine
9. Egypt, abandoned, Paris
10. Elba, Waterloo, St. Helena

Chronology

1. Boston Tea Party: 1773
2. Declaration of American Independence: 1776
3. Storming of the Bastille: 1789
4. American Bill of Rights: 1791
5. Louis XVI executed: 1793
6. Continental System: 1806
7. Battle of Waterloo: 1815

CHAPTER 20

Matching

1. D
2. E
3. H
4. A
5. F
6. I
7. G
8. B
9. C
10. J

Multiple Choice

1. c
2. b
3. a
4. d
5. b
6. a
7. d
8. d
9. b
10. b
11. c
12. d
13. a
14. b
15. c
16. d
17. a
18. b
19. c
20. b

Completion

1. Coal, iron, rivers, size
2. Arkwright, Cartwright
3. Locomotive, *Rocket*
4. Crystal Palace, Kensington, Britain
5. Coal, Ruhr, Rhineland
6. Catholic, Protestant, potato
7. Poor Law, atmospheric, sanitation
8. Size, broken, cheap
9. Males, paid, annually
10. Twelve, nine, reading, arithmetic

Chronology

1. Watt's rotary steam engine: 1782
2. Cartwright's power loom: 1787
3. Trevithick's steam locomotive: 1804
4. Combination Acts repealed: 1824
5. People's Charter: 1838
6. Ten Hours Act: 1847
7. Great Exhibition: 1851

CHAPTER 21

Matching

1. D
2. H
3. A
4. J
5. F
6. B
7. I
8. C
9. G
10. E

Multiple Choice

1. b
2. c
3. a
4. c
5. d
6. d
7. a
8. d
9. b
10. a
11. c
12. d
13. d
14. c
15. a
16. c
17. c
18. d
19. b
20. a

Completion

1. Metternich, Castlereagh, Talleyrand
2. Simón Bolivar, Monroe Doctrine
3. Russia, France, Britain, independent
4. Decembrist Revolt, Secret Police
5. Thomas Malthus, David Ricardo
6. Phalansteries, New Lanark, New Harmony
7. Feminism, absolute equality
8. Louis-Philippe, Louis Napoleon Bonaparte
9. Debelleyme, serjents, cane, saber
10. Walter Scott, Mary Shelley

Chronology

1. Wars of Independence in Latin America begin: 1819
2. Greek revolt against the Turks begins: 1821
3. Decembrist Revolt in Russia: 1825
4. July Revolution in France: 1830
5. British Reform Act: 1832
6. Repeal of Corn Laws in Britain: 1846
7. Revolts or revolutions in France, Germany, Italy, and Austria: 1848

CHAPTER 22

Matching

1. E
2. H
3. A
4. J
5. B
6. F
7. I
8. D
9. C
10. G

Multiple Choice

1. a
2. d
3. d
4. c
5. d
6. a
7. b
8. d
9. b
10. a
11. c
12. d
13. b
14. c
15. b
16. a
17. a
18. b
19. c
20. d

Completion

1. Ottoman, Crimean, Britain, Concert
2. *Risorgimento*, Victor Emmanuel II, Savoy
3. Denmark, Austria, France, Empire
4. Land, marry, assassination
5. Disraeli, Liberal
6. Jewish rabbis, Protestant, atheism
7. *Communist Manifesto*, proletariat, bourgeoisie, classless
8. South, South, *Beagle*
9. Romantic, adultery, suicide
10. German, Nibelung

Chronology

1. Second French Empire proclaimed: 1852
2. Russian Emancipation Edict: 1861
3. American Civil War ends: 1865
4. Austro-Prussian War: 1866
5. British Reform Act: 1867
6. Italy annexes Rome: 1870
7. German Empire proclaimed: 1871

CHAPTER 23

Matching

1. F
2. I
3. C
4. E
5. A
6. H
7. B
8. J
9. D
10. G

Multiple Choice

1. a
2. c
3. a
4. d
5. c
6. a
7. b
8. a
9. d
10. c
11. a
12. b
13. c
14. b
15. d
16. a
17. c
18. d
19. b
20. c

Completion

1. Innovations, technical
2. White collar, teaching, nursing
3. Marxism, French Revolution
4. 21, 147, 40, 80
5. London, Liverpool, private enterprise
6. Condoms, diaphragms
7. Moral, civic, secular
8. Commune, shot, penal colony
9. Junker, monarchy, aristocracy, emperor
10. Secret police, martial law

Chronology

1. Paris Commune: 1871
2. Spanish constitution: 1875
3. Bismarck's antisocialist law: 1878
4. Irish Land Act: 1881
5. Jacob's Clinic: 1882
6. British Housing Act: 1890
7. Bernstein's *Socialism* published: 1899

CHAPTER 24

Matching

1. G
2. I
3. D
4. F
5. E
6. H
7. A
8. J
9. B
10. C

Multiple Choice

1. a
2. b
3. c
4. a
5. a
6. d
7. c
8. c
9. d
10. b
11. b
12. c
13. d
14. a
15. b
16. c
17. c
18. d
19. d
20. a

Completion

1. Quanta, atoms, Isaac Newton
2. Relativity, observer, time, space
3. Unconscious, oblivious, dreams
4. Darwinism, war, biological
5. Property, capitalism, socialism, Marxism
6. Impression, light, modern
7. Asia, Africa, penetration
8. Transvaal, Orange Free State, British
9. Boxers, Sun Yat-sen, Manchu
10. Meiji, Chinese, Korea, Russia

Chronology

1. British take Hong Kong: 1842
2. Suez Canal opened: 1869
3. Three Emperors' League formed: 1873
4. Victoria crowned Empress of India: 1876
5. Boxer Rebellion in China: 1900-1901
6. Triple Entente formed: 1907
7. Japan annexes Korea: 1910

CHAPTER 25

Matching

1. J
2. D
3. G
4. A
5. I
6. B
7. E
8. C
9. H
10. F

Multiple Choice

1. a
2. c
3. b
4. b
5. a
6. d
7. c
8. a
9. a
10. b
11. a
12. d
13. c
14. a
15. b
16. d
17. d
18. a
19. b
20. c

Completion

1. Irish, Poles, Slavs
2. Bosnian, Serbian, Black Head
3. Joffre, Marne, trench
4. Verdun, Somme, Champagne
5. Shell, salary, explodes
6. 1917, submarine warfare
7. Hindenburg, Ludendorff, total war
8. Prime Minister, class
9. Provisional, Bolsheviks, Lenin
10. Fourteen Points, Britain, France

Chronology

1. Francis Ferdinand assassinated: June, 1914
2. World War 1 begins: August, 1914
3. U.S. enters the war: April, 1917
4. Treaty of Brest-Litovsk: March, 1918
5. Second Battle of Marne: July, 1918
6. Armistice: November, 1918
7. Paris Conference begins: January, 1919

CHAPTER 26

Matching

1. G
2. I
3. B
4. J
5. A
6. C
7. H
8. D
9. E
10. F

Multiple Choice

1. c
2. a
3. b
4. c
5. d
6. b
7. c
8. b
9. d
10. b
11. c
12. a
13. b
14. a
15. d
16. d
17. c
18. b
19. c
20. a

Completion

1. League, Nations, France, Germany
2. Reparations, Ruhr, inflation
3. Demand, public works, deficit spending
4. Working, New Deal
5. Elementary school, *Avanti*, Fascist
6. Jews, Heinrich Himmler, Hitler Youth
7. Bolsheviks, Leon Trotsky, Mexico
8. *Dopolavoro*, *Kraft durch Freude*
9. Purposelessness, anti-art, Surrealist
10. *Ulysses*, consciousness, Dublin

Chronology

1. Fascist dictatorship established in Italy: 1925
2. Stalin dictatorship begins in Russia: 1929
3. National Government begins in Britain: 1931
4. New Deal begins in the U.S.: 1933
5. Hitler dictatorship begins in Germany: 1934
6. Popular Front formed in France: 1936
7. *Kristallnacht* in Germany: 1938

CHAPTER 27

Matching

1. J
2. D
3. B
4. F
5. H
6. A
7. I
8. C
9. G
10. E

Multiple Choice

1. b
2. b
3. d
4. c
5. a
6. b
7. b
8. a
9. c
10. b
11. c
12. a
13. c
14. d
15. c
16. a
17. b
18. d
19. c
20. d

Completion

1. Rhineland, Austria, weak
2. Appeasement, Czechoslovakia
3. Poland, *blitzkrieg*, France
4. Pétain, Vichy
5. China, Indochina, Pearl Harbor
6. North Africa, Stalingrad, Coral Sea
7. Communists, Rose, Gestapo
8. Madagascar, Reinhard Heydrich, annihilation
9. Russia, Night Witches
10. American, Hiroshima, Nagasaki

Chronology

1. German occupation of Rhineland: March 7, 1936
2. German invasion of Poland: September 1, 1939
3. Battle of Britain: Fall, 1940
4. Japanese attack Pearl Harbor: December 7, 1941
5. German surrender at Stalingrad: February 2, 1943
6. Allied invasion of France: June 6, 1944
7. U.S. drops atomic bombs on Japan: August 8, 1945

CHAPTER 28

Matching

1. D
2. I
3. G
4. A
5. C
6. B
7. E
8. J
9. F
10. H

Multiple Choice

1. a
2. b
3. d
4. b
5. c
6. b
7. c
8. a
9. a
10. c
11. c
12. a
13. b
14. d
15. b
16. a
17. c
18. c
19. b
20. d

Completion

1. British, Greece, Turkey
2. Soviet, *Foreign Affairs*, containment
3. Missiles, blockade, invade
4. Philippines, India, Indochina
5. First World, Second World, Third World
6. Stalin, satellites, Hungary, Czechoslovakia
7. NATO, nuclear, automobiles, armaments
8. "Economic miracle," Konrad Adenauer
9. Bank, Insurance, Health
10. Homosexuality, education, contraception

Chronology

1. Truman Doctrine: 1947
2. Formation of NATO: 1949
3. Formation of the Warsaw Pact: 1955
4. De Gaulle assumes power in France: 1958
5. Erection of Berlin Wall: 1961
6. Cuban Missile Crisis: 1962
7. Prague Spring: 1968

CHAPTER 29

Matching

1. J
2. D
3. G
4. A
5. I
6. B
7. H
8. C
9. F
10. E

Multiple Choice

1. b
2. c
3. a
4. d
5. c
6. b
7. d
8. a
9. c
10. b
11. d
12. a
13. b
14. c
15. d
16. b
17. a
18. c
19. c
20. b

Completion

1. Evil empire, Star Wars
2. Kuwait, Gulf
3. Solidarity, labor, Lech Walesa
4. Ethnic, Nazi, 250,000
5. Unemployment, taxes, foreign
6. Labor unions, inflation, Falklands
7. Aldo Moro, Red Brigades
8. Chernobyl, Environment
9. Samuel Beckett, *Waiting for Godot*
10. Death, destiny, himself

Chronology

1. Thatcher becomes British Prime Minister: 1979
2. Solidarity Movement emerges in Poland: 1980
3. Mitterand elected President of France: 1981
4. Kohl chosen Chancellor of West Germany: 1982
5. Gorbachev comes to power in U.S.S.R.: 1985
6. Reunification of Germany: 1990
7. Dissolution of U.S.S.R.: 1991